So You Want To Be A Writer

Allison Tait

Valerie Khoo

Published by Australian Writers' Centre Publishing
An imprint of the Australian Writers' Centre
Suite 3, 55 Lavender Street, Milsons Point NSW 2061
Ph: +612 9929 0088
www.writerscentre.com.au

The moral right of the authors has been asserted.

For quantity sales or media enquiries, please contact the publisher
books@writerscentre.com.au

 A catalogue record for this
book is available from the
NATIONAL
LIBRARY National Library of Australia
OF AUSTRALIA

ISBN: 978-0-6485559-0-2 (paperback)
         978-0-6485559-1-9 (ebook)

Editing: Nigel Bartlett
Cover Design: Valerie Khoo and Bronte Whittle
Formatting: Author Secret
Publishing Consultant: Linda Diggle

Disclaimer: Although the authors and publisher have made every effort to
ensure the information in this book was correct at press time, the authors
and publisher do not assume and hereby disclaim any liability to any party
for any loss, damage, or disruption caused by errors or omissions, whether
such errors or omissions result from negligence, accident, or any other cause.

For everyone who ever said 'yes'

Contents

Introduction

So you want to be a writer.

Chances are you've been thinking about this for a long time. Writing is something you did when you were a kid. Or it was one of your best subjects at school.

Perhaps this is something that's crept up on you, the feeling that writing is something you should be doing, that you *need* to be doing.

Maybe you've even started, secretly opening a document called 'My novel' and beginning to write – and then getting nowhere, flummoxed by what to do next. Or maybe you read the weekend papers or your favourite website and think, "I could write something like that!"

If so, you're in the right place.

This book is designed to help you to take that whisper, that need, that desire to write, and turn it into something practical.

This is not a book about the craft of writing. There are lots and lots of courses and books out there to teach you the skills you need as a writer. Courses about structure and sentences. Books about hooks and climaxes, plotting and pacing. Workshops on the art of copywriting and on how to get more clients.

We recommend you sign up to those workshops and read those books – as many as you can find – and do those courses. Learn everything you can about the craft of writing.

But be aware that all the writing skills in the world won't matter if you don't know what to do with them. They won't help if you don't know how to use your talent and knowledge to get you from A (where you are now) to B (the writing career of your dreams).

This book addresses all the other things you need to do to achieve your writing goals.

We won't tell you how or what to write. But we can tell you how to be a writer.

We'll look at how to decide what kind of writer you want to be. Where to find ideas, and what to do with them. How to get a book written. How to build a writing business. How to transition into a writing career. And more.

So who are we?

Regular listeners of our top-rating *So You Want To Be A Writer* podcast will know us well. In fact, with over one million downloads since the podcast began, there are thousands and thousands of listeners out there who know #ValandAl, as we're known, possibly a little too well!

They'll know that Valerie Khoo is the founder and CEO of the Australian Writers' Centre, the country's leading centre for writing courses. She has a publishing career stretching over 20 years that includes roles as a writer, journalist and editor. Valerie is author of the book *Power Stories: The 8 Stories You Must Tell to Build an Epic Business* – as well as countless magazine and newspaper articles – and has a no-nonsense approach to the business of writing.

They'll also know that Val has a penchant for banoffee pie, a menagerie of pets and a singular passion for Jon Bon Jovi. Her Word of the Week segment on the podcast is a highlight (for Val – but not so much for Al…). And more recently, she's added another string to her bow and is now a visual artist and arts/culture festival curator.

Allison Tait, meanwhile, is the internationally published, bestselling author of two epic, middle-grade adventure series: *The Mapmaker Chronicles* and the *Ateban Cipher*.

With decades of experience in publishing, both as an editor and a writer, and with two non-fiction books, two ghost-written books and several (unpublished) adult manuscripts to her name, Al's gone from full-time freelance writer to children's author, creative writing teacher and in-demand speaker. Our podcast community has listened in as she's taken that journey.

Her busy family life, writing companion Procrastipup, wardrobe of authorial blazers and overriding philosophy of "finish the damn book" also get regular airtime.

We met in 1998 when we were both working for *Cleo* magazine.

We won't bore you here with our writing CVs (see the end of this book for the official breakdown), because this book is not about us.

It's about you.

It's about you taking that dream of being a writer and turning it into a reality.

So You Want To Be A Writer is a beginner's guide for people who want to be writers. Like all good non-fiction books, we've broken it into sections so you can dip in and out as needed or read it from start to finish.

We'll walk you through each stage, from deciding what kind of writer you want to be (don't laugh, this is a big question!), where to get ideas and how to share your writing dream with other people. We'll take you through how to get the words written, finding your writing community (and why you need one), harnessing your creativity, how to use technology and the business of being a writer.

We've drawn together the best advice we've found from our many interviews with some of the world's most successful writers. You'll read tips about the writing process, getting the first publishing deal, dealing with editors, writing the book and everything in between, by authors such as Liane Moriarty, Michael Robotham, Nick Earls, Charlotte Wood, Graeme Simsion, Jane Harper, Di Morrissey, Anita Heiss, Garry Disher, Jaclyn Moriarty, Andy Griffiths, Amie Kaufman, Jackie French, Veronica Roth and more.

Literary authors, commercial fiction authors, non-fiction authors, publishers, agents, crime authors, romance authors, children's authors, young adult authors, freelance writers, content writers – you name it, we've got them, Australian and international.

This is a masterclass in writing and an incredible resource in itself.

So what are you waiting for?

If you want to be a writer, the time to start is now!

CHAPTER 1
Ready to be a writer?

Picture this. You're sitting at your computer tapping away at the keys, ideas pouring out of your brain so fast that your fingers can't keep up. Maybe you're working on your next piece of writing – a story that's been swirling around your brain for ages – and finally it's forming right there on the screen in front of you.

Your characters are coming to life, the story is so intriguing that you can't even wait for the next paragraph to emerge, and you feel such an outpouring of creativity that you simply can't stop. You're in a creative flow. And it feels like magic.

It's the dream, right?

If this is your idea of an idyllic way to spend the day, you might be wondering if this is ever going to happen. Or whether it will remain in your fantasies forever.

Well, the good news for you is that this is not a movie. It's real life. And if you're reading this book, chances are that you're interested in the life of a writer.

Maybe you're not quite sure what kind of writer you want to be – novelist, freelance writer, content writer, copywriter, the list goes on. On the other hand, maybe you're crystal clear on your writing aspirations. It doesn't matter where you are on your writing journey – or even if you haven't even started on it. Because this book will give you the inspiration, motivation and guidance to help you on your path.

Also, we know that not everyone has the luxury of writing full-time when they start out. In fact, most people begin their writing careers as a side hustle.

You might work in an unrelated field, but perhaps you've always harboured a secret love of words that you want to explore. Or maybe you already write in some form at work, but want to indulge in personal writing projects in your spare time.

Whatever your situation, we get it. You probably have a day job. So this book is about how you can follow your writing dreams when you have other commitments. It's about how to foster your creativity, even if you're focused on another professional career.

It's about being able to have your cake and eat it too. Despite the old saying that this is not possible, it is.

As long as you follow some simple rules.

Rule 1: You need to believe it's possible

The first step in making this a reality is acknowledging that you can do it. After all, if you suspect that it will be a pipe dream – if you think this is something that only ever happens to other people – then it's likely that perception will become your reality.

We know that sounds a bit 'woo woo', but if you want the cold hard truth, it's this: until you believe that you can pursue your dream of becoming a writer, it will never be in your grasp.

Right now, some of you are thinking, "Well, I'd better stop reading here then." Because, deep down, you don't think it's possible.

It's very easy – and perfectly natural – to think this way. We're conditioned by our families to take the safe option. That is, to follow traditional career paths that lead to secure jobs, not realising those jobs could disappear in a single decision by management.

We're conditioned by our peers not to take risks that are too big. Because we could fail. Or we could risk disappointment.

We're conditioned to think that dreams come true for *other* people. Why on earth would they happen to us?

The thing is, all of these sentiments usually come from well-meaning loved ones. But the irony is that, if we heed them, we could end up never realising our potential, never experiencing the joy of achieving our goals, and never expressing the creative voice that's in each and every one of us.

So, while it might not come naturally to you, it's vital to believe that pursuing your creative dreams – and achieving them – is possible. Because once you believe that, you've already won half the battle. And that's pretty exciting!

Author Terry Pratchett is known for saying: "The first draft is just you telling yourself the story." He's referring to the first draft of a manuscript and his point is that you should just be telling yourself the story of your characters and what happens to them. That first draft shouldn't necessarily be about writing what your readers want or crafting a story to other people's expectations.

However, his quote goes deeper than that. It can also refer to the story you tell yourself... *about yourself*. If you fundamentally tell yourself the story that it's too hard to become a writer, that will become your reality. If you don't think you can succeed, that story will underpin how your life turns out. But if you tell yourself the story that you can explore and thrive as a writer, you're shaping the story that you'll get to live.

If you still need convincing, stick with us. We hope that the stories in this book of creatives (with day jobs) can show you that your goals are within your grasp.

Rule 2: It starts off as a side hustle

When you want to pursue a creative endeavour, success almost always starts off as a side hustle. Especially if you're exploring your creative side later in life.

By that time, you might have a family, mortgage and other responsibilities you need to commit time and money to – so a writing side hustle is your only option to start with.

But that shouldn't be considered a negative. While you might like the idea of winning the lottery so you have the luxury of spending all morning writing and then all afternoon drinking tea and musing about what lyrical prose you've just penned, the truth is that some people find this situation more of a curse than a blessing.

Why? Because there's no imperative to succeed. There's no need to be efficient. There's no urgency to learn and create opportunities. When you start your writing career as a side hustle, you have to make every minute count. And that means you need to make decisions and grab opportunities that will give you the best return on your efforts.

Nurturing a side hustle is also less risky. We know very few people who will say: "Hey, I'm going to give up my hefty salary tomorrow so I can transform myself overnight into a writer earning the equivalent income!"

Very few people go down this path because it's simply not a wise decision, especially if you have big family expenses to consider or loans you need to pay back.

However, we do know tonnes of people who take a stepped approach. That is, their writing starts off as a side hustle, perhaps after hours or on weekends. When they get some runs on the board, then they devote more time to it.

Tamsin's side hustle led to award-winning books

Award-winning author Tamsin Janu is a good example. When Tamsin first ventured into the world of writing, she was studying law at university. During a weekend course at the Australian Writers' Centre, she came up with the idea for her first book, *Figgy in the World*, about a little girl named Figgy in the West African country of Ghana. Aimed at eight to 12-year-olds, the book won a slew of awards and established Tamsin as a fresh, exciting voice in publishing.

Tamsin says, "Seeing it in bookstores was definitely a thrill, as was other people telling me they'd bought or read it. I still receive emails from kids telling me how much they liked the book and asking really detailed questions about the story. It's great they're so interested!"

After graduating from law, Tamsin entered the workforce and another couple of books followed: *Figgy and the President* and *Figgy Takes the City*. While working at a legal association four days a week, Tamsin dedicated the fifth day to her writing side hustle. She has since released another novel, *Blossom*, a fantasy-mystery set in Australia that follows the adventures of 10-year-old Lottie.

Tamsin shows that a side hustle can result in publishing success. She doesn't work full-time as a writer, but instead fits her writing around her lifestyle and other commitments. "How much I get done, or whether I get any done at all, varies widely from week to week," she admits.

Incorporating her passion for writing into her life has paid off. "I still feel kind of overwhelmed seeing my name listed alongside really great and established Australian children's authors."

Brad went from history teacher to full-time writer

Brad Kelly was in a successful career as a history teacher for 15 years before he decided to explore his love for writing. Brad completed several courses at the Australian Writers' Centre while working full-time in teaching.

He wanted to give his side hustle a go, so he quit his full-time teaching job and worked a few days per week as a casual teacher while building up his freelance writing career. Within a year, his side hustle became a healthy full-time income. Brad took a stepped approach and it worked.

"I do a variety of work for corporates, for content writing, for book publishers and for private contracts and commissions," says Brad.

"Being in the Australian Writers' Centre community taught me that making a living from writing is absolutely possible. Writing is a business and the AWC masterclass program has helped me treat it as such. I have spreadsheets, financial targets and a business plan. It opened up a whole world of ideas that I wouldn't have been previously exposed to."

After hours activities

When your writing starts off as a side hustle, you have to work at it after hours or on weekends if you want to grow it. Sometimes that means writing when you're tired, or while you're waiting for the kids at soccer, or getting up earlier so you can write a few hundred words before everyone else gets up.

We met a woman recently who said, "I love writing. I know I'll find a publisher for my novel when I finally finish it because it's got a really great plot. But it's just so hard to find the time."

She went on to tell us how her day job was so mentally taxing that the last thing she felt like doing after she got home was to sit in front of her computer to write her great story.

Her job may well be mentally taxing. So might yours. But if you want your writing to progress beyond being a nice little fantasy, you need to be serious about your side hustle.

Nigel's Sunday writing sessions

Nigel Bartlett took that approach. He had a busy day job but also had a compelling story brewing in his brain for years. So he decided to commit his Sundays to writing it. That meant turning down social functions and invites from friends, and not allowing himself to go hang out in the park, gym or shops.

He designated that time to writing and, for the most part, stuck to it. "Usually I write on a Sunday," Nigel says. "If I get invited to any social engagement on that day I just say, 'Sorry, that's my writing day.' Going to the beach and that sort of thing is out of the question on my Sundays."

Nigel's Sunday sessions resulted in his page-turning debut novel *King of the Road*, and he was over the moon when it was shortlisted for a Ned Kelly crime fiction award.

Rule 3: Follow the steps in this book

We're laying out a blueprint for you right here in this book. If you follow the advice we're giving you, based on literally decades of our experience – not to mention the generous tips from all the authors we've featured – you will get there.

We get pretty excited when we see aspiring writers follow this blueprint and find success. It makes us do our own respective happy dances. Allison's is likely to be a shimmy against the strains of a bluesy jazz number, while Valerie's is probably a vigorous boogie to Bon Jovi. (Yes, we're unashamed dags but we're okay with that.)

The point is that it really does warm the cockles of our hearts when we see people achieve their writing dreams. And we're not even a tiny bit smug if they get there because they've followed our blueprint. Okay we can't lie... maybe just a *tiny* bit smug.

But here's the thing, it's called a blueprint for a reason. It lays out the various components and foundations that will lead you towards becoming the writer you want to be. And they're all important.

Blueprints and building plans are vital when you're constructing a house. If you ignore the section that tells you where the supporting walls are going to be, you may end up with some semblance of a house – but it won't stand for very long.

The same goes for our blueprint. If you choose to ignore some of the key elements because you think they're not important or that they don't apply to you, you're not giving yourself the best chance of success. Or you'll simply take longer to get there.

We're sharing this blueprint with you because we want you to achieve your own personal writing goals. And, we'll be honest, we get asked how to do this so many times every week that we figured the most efficient way to reach as many people as possible was to lay out the blueprint in this book in a way that's easy for anyone to follow.

The key word here is "follow". Sure, you can cherry pick the bits that sound most appealing to you – and that will help you make *some* progress. However, if you follow our blueprint step by step, you'll maximise your opportunities and fast-track your quest to becoming a writer.

Okay, are you ready for your first few steps?

We know that if you've picked up this book, you're probably interested in writing. But perhaps you're not sure what your first steps should be. When you Google "how to become a writer", so many options come up that it's hard to know which one is the best path for your needs. So which direction should you head in?

In the next chapter, you'll discover exactly that.

CHAPTER 2
Your first few steps into the world of writing

When you experience that first inkling that you want to explore the world of writing, it can be challenging to know where to start. There are so many options, so many Facebook ads telling you about masterclasses that will turn you into a published author and so many opinions from friends and family on what they think you should do.

It's certainly something that Valerie experienced when she first ventured into the world of writing. While Allison began her career as a writer early on, working her way from secretary to cadet journalist by the age of 19, Valerie came to writing via a circuitous route.

In fact, her first career could not have been further from the world of writing. She became… wait for it… an accountant! We know. It's hard to believe, but it's true. More about that later!

Both of us know what it feels like to have that creative urge to explore the world of writing. And if you're feeling that urge now, we strongly encourage you to give in to it.

We know it can be scary to admit you have this secret passion to become a writer. We know it can even be confronting, especially when you're in a whole other career, one you've spent years studying for, or one you've invested time in and built to a decent level.

Allison will tell you that, even as a working journalist, making the switch to writing fiction felt like a leap of faith. "It felt like such a big thing, to say to other people, 'I'm writing a novel,'" she says. "Like, 'Who am I to be trying to do this?'"

Deep down, some people are scared that if they open the door to the world of writing, they could discover they've made the wrong decisions about their career up until this point. And they're concerned that it's now too late to start again with a new one. So they leave that door firmly shut, in case they realise they're missing out on what they're truly meant to do in life.

These are normal fears. *Completely normal.*

But we want to make it clear that giving in to your creative curiosity about writing doesn't mean you need to change your life in any kind of dramatic fashion. It doesn't automatically mean you're going to chuck in your current vocation and begin a new life as a writer tomorrow – to hell with the consequences.

You don't have to suddenly throw caution to the wind, give up your day job and plunge headfirst into an uncertain new career in writing. Nooooo. That's not a pathway we advise. Remember, we reckon that writing usually starts off as a side hustle.

15

If these kinds of thoughts are anywhere on your radar, you're projecting waaaay too far into the future. Don't overthink it.

Just treat that little voice inside you that's nudging you into the world of writing as a good friend who wants you to be happy.

Go on, flirt a little

If you're wondering whether you should entertain the thought of writing as a side hustle, then we suggest you simply treat it as a brief exploration. A flirtation of sorts. You know, a simple glance, a little hello, a brief encounter where there are no strings attached.

It's like the coffee you have with someone who piques your interest before you decide whether you want to turn it into a full-blown romance.

What does that look like in real life? Well, it depends on what works for you, but here are some possible first steps:

- **Journalling**: If you're interested in the idea of writing but don't actually… write… then start journalling regularly to see what it feels like to have words pour out of your brain, through your fingers and onto the page (or keyboard).

  In *The Artist's Way*, Julia Cameron advocates doing "morning pages". These are three pages of longhand writing in which you allow yourself to write in a stream of consciousness fashion, knowing that no-one is going to read what you write except for you.

  There'll be no judgement, no expectations and no pressure that you need to create anything that's publishable or even decipherable. As long as you do it every day and let yourself write whatever comes into your head, this process can provide you with great clarity on what's truly important to you in life. It also gets you into the habit of writing regularly.

- **Do a short course:** You don't have to commit to a three-year degree. Or even a one-year program of study. Start off small. Do a weekend workshop. If you're too much of a commitment-phobe even to do that, then enrol in an online workshop that you could complete in a few hours.

  Some people think the only way for them to truly explore their love of writing is to gain an academic qualification. However, the beauty of writing is that unlike a profession like medicine or engineering, you don't need a piece of paper to show you have the goods. Writing is one of those skills that can be honed without a heavy-duty tertiary qualification. So don't get hung up on the idea that you need to get one.

- **Enter a short story competition:** You don't have to embark on an 80,000-word novel as your first project. Write a short story. Write some flash fiction of only 500 words. Enter competitions without putting any pressure on yourself that you need to win! Just enjoy the act of writing.

We're sure you can think of other brief flirtations that can connect you into the world of writing. Even if it's simply trying your hand at *The New Yorker*'s caption competition, where readers are invited to pen their own captions to an illustration each week. Just do *something*.

These small actions give you a taste for what it feels like to write. Because the mere act of writing will eventually reveal to you the steps you should take next.

You'll find that you gravitate to certain types of writing. You'll be more passionate about certain genres or style and less interested in others. But you'll never discover this if you just read the theory about different types of writing. It's in the actual 'doing' that you discover what really sparks your interest.

What if you find out you love it?

Let's say you do this for a while and realise, "Yes, I love to write!" And you want to take this further but you're not sure what to do next.

If you think this might be a direction you want to continue in, this is where we strongly encourage you to do a course. And not just because we both teach courses in writing!

It's because we don't want you to waste time. There's no doubt that if you do a course, you'll fast-track your learning. In a short time, you'll learn rules, techniques and vital industry information that would otherwise take years to glean.

Let's take one of our students, Greg. He worked on his novels for years and years. But he beavered away in isolation, writing at every available opportunity, fleshing out his characters and taking them on an epic adventure. Greg ended up with a multi-book series.

He even hired editors and manuscript assessors to polish his massive tome. We could see he had a passion for storytelling and the seed of a great idea. But Greg, who worked in a day job as an engineer, had never learnt the fundamentals of creative writing through any kind of course or book or workshop. Sure, he read fiction a lot – but that isn't the same as actually honing his skills in writing. Even though we tried to convince him to do a course, it was years before he finally did so.

And in Greg's words: "I wish I'd done this sooner. *You don't know what you don't know.* And I could have saved a lot of time if I'd learnt some of the basic rules of writing and publishing way back when I was still writing my first manuscript. Doing a course was one of the most valuable things I could have done for my writing – not only because of what I've learnt, but also because I've realised how valuable it is to be around other writers."

Greg touches on another important part of your journey into writing. It's important to be part of a community. That is, people who understand what it's like to journey down the path of becoming a writer. If you can't access an entire community, then at least find a handful of friends who share the same passion as you do.

That's because writing can be an isolating activity. You're always in your head or tapping away at your computer. And even if you're usually quite a loner, it can do wonders for your writing – not to mention your sanity – if you can connect with other people who are going through the same experiences you're going through.

You don't have to throw in your day job!

Now, you might be perfectly happy in your current job – and that's great! We're certainly not here to tell you to quit it. Not at all. Many people are happy to stick with their chosen careers and enjoy writing as a sideline. We've had many students successfully do just that. They enjoy earning a part-time income from writing – whether that's writing books or freelance articles – and because they have a full-time income from their day job, they don't feel any pressure to earn a certain income level from their writing.

They literally do it for the love of it. Many confess they love it so much they'd even do it if they didn't get paid. The income is simply a bonus – a reward where they get paid to explore an interest they're passionate about.

They're part of the growing number of multi-hyphenates who successfully juggle dual professions.

But you can if you want

However, perhaps you're now at the stage where you actually want to transition out of your career to become a writer. Perhaps your flirtation with writing has revealed that you're not in a very happy relationship with your current job. And you think you might want out.

That's totally understandable. It can be easy to be seduced into this new career if you're miserable with your current one. And if you're truly passionate about writing, then we want to encourage you every step of the way.

We're not going to lie. It's not like you're going to do one course, snap your fingers and become a fully fledged writer overnight. You're going to have to put in some work. But if you're prepared to do it, we truly believe that you can make it.

"What?" we hear some of you exclaim. "How can you be so sure? You don't even know us. We've bought your book, but you really don't know our personal circumstances."

That may be true. We may never have met you. And, to be clear, we're not saying writing is such an amazing profession that it's going to transcend all your problems and provide you with a fairytale ending to your life.

Do what you love – and the money will follow

We do have one mantra that we believe from the bottom of our hearts. That is: do what you love – and the money will follow.

It's faith in this mantra that gave Valerie the push to move out of her former career. "It was a big decision to quit my career in accounting, but I was miserable," she says.

"Even though I had great peers, a wonderful employer and opportunities to work overseas, I'd feel physically sick every Sunday night because I knew I had to go to work the next day.

"It seemed ridiculous and it was hard for the people around me to understand because, on paper, it looked like I was in a great job. And I was. It just wasn't a great job for me."

Valerie says that doing courses was instrumental in helping her to transition into the world of writing.

"Courses helped me to hone my craft and take myself seriously as a writer," she says. "The skills I learnt from those courses gave me the confidence to really consider writing as a possible alternative to what I was doing.

"I had this romantic notion that, when it comes to your career, you should do what you love – and the money will follow.

"The reality is that if you love what you do, you'll become great at it. And when you're great at something, people notice and more opportunities come your way."

When Valerie left her career in accounting, she became a public relations consultant. "That was certainly a more creative outlet than working in accounting. And I thought I'd be able to satisfy my urge to write within a PR environment and doing some freelance writing for magazines on the side.

"That worked for a while, but then I got that nagging feeling inside me again, nudging me to explore the idea of writing full-time. I knew I had to do something about it or I'd be forever wondering, 'What if?'"

Valerie asked herself what her dream job would be. "Without hesitation, I knew I wanted to work as a writer on a glossy magazine. I grew up working part-time in a newsagency and I'd pore over the magazines every single week and imagine myself being one of the names on the masthead."

So she embarked on a campaign to find that dream job, contacting magazines and simply sending in her résumé. "I finally received a response from the editor of a magazine saying she was happy to meet me for an interview. I fell off my chair."

After the interview, the editor called Valerie in for another meeting. "She started telling me that she felt I might not want the role because it would mean a big pay cut from the salary level I was on as a senior PR consultant. I thought she was letting me down gently. But eventually I realised that she was offering me the job!

"I didn't care about the salary. I just knew this was my dream job and every fibre of my being wanted it."

While it's true that this meant a huge pay cut for Valerie, she still believed in the mantra: do what you love – and the money will follow.

"When I first took the job, it was challenging financially," she says. "But within six months I was asked to be deputy editor at another glossy magazine at double the salary. So while I did have to sacrifice in the short-term, it definitely paid off not long after that. Do what you love – and the money will follow."

So what's YOUR path?

We mentioned that we're going to provide you with a blueprint to becoming a writer. What does that look like? In the rest of this book, we'll discuss the steps you need to take.

It all starts with working out what kind of writer you want to be…

CHAPTER 3
What kind of writer do you want to be?

The word *writer* is incredibly broad. But think of it as an umbrella term for a whole range of different types of writers, each with their own specific skills and creative output. While this list is by no means exhaustive, we're highlighting the main writing careers most people consider.

This is important because there are many misconceptions out there about what each of these writers do. So it's useful to get the terminology right.

For example, it's common for people to tell us, "We want to do a creative writing course because we want to be able to write more creatively." But when we delve further into what they really want, we discover they want to write their company's annual reports in a way that engages and connects with their shareholders. The reality is that they need to improve their skills in clear and concise corporate communication – they don't need to do a creative writing course.

Understanding what defines different types of writers will help you go for the right opportunities and bypass the ones that won't help you achieve your goal.

The creative writer

This in itself is a broad term but when people do "creative writing", typically, this refers to fiction writers. That is, people who write novels for adults or children, or picture books. Some memoir writers also consider themselves creative writers.

The writers in this category often have a day job to start with, because writing a novel is a long process. Sometimes it can take years to get your first novel off the ground.

However, even successful authors who've published several books sometimes keep their day jobs simply because they love the structure that it brings while they wrangle an entire novel into shape.

Like bestselling author Karen Viggers, author of several books including *The Lightkeeper's Wife*, who has sold over 800,000 books. She still works one day a week as a wildlife vet because she loves it.

Or Joanna Nell, author of *The Single Ladies of Jacaranda Retirement Village*, who combines her work as a doctor with writing novels. Joanna initially explored the world of writing when an unexpected accident meant she was laid up in bed for six weeks. During that time, she enrolled in a creative writing course at the Australian Writers' Centre.

"I enrolled in Creative Writing Stage 1 when I was wrangling a full-time career as a GP, as well as being a taxi service and personal assistant to two teenagers. I was in my mid-forties and, like every busy parent, simply trying to get through to Friday without crashing. I did very little for myself and had few hobbies beyond reading and ironing.

"The course was the absolute nuts and bolts approach I was looking for. I loved the logical step-by-step approach to the craft of writing. It sounds strange but although I'd been a voracious reader all my life, I'd never stopped to consider how a book was actually written, or even that it was divided into a series of scenes with a defined structure. It's obvious now, but at the time I thought I'd discovered radium.

"At 52, however, I like to think I'm taking the advice that's at the heart of *The Single Ladies of Jacaranda Retirement Village*, which is:

"It's never too late to live the life you've always dreamt of."

The freelance writer

This is another broad term. Typically, it refers to someone who writes articles for magazines, newspapers and online publications. Copywriters and content writers can sometimes also refer to themselves as freelance writers.

In fact, the lines are blurring between freelance writers, copywriters and content writers – largely because more and more people choose to do a combination of two or three of these.

However, for the purposes of this book, when we refer to freelance writers, we mean the people who write for publications like *The Sydney Morning Herald*, *Q Weekend*, *Body + Soul*, *MindFood*, *marie claire*, *Essential Kids*, *Acuity* (which is the magazine for members of the Institute of Chartered Accountants), *Voyeur* (the inflight magazine for Virgin Airlines), *Jones* (the David Jones magazine) and many others in print and online.

You'll see that there are many and varied publications that use freelance writers and it's impossible for us to list them all. But chances are that if you want to write an article for a magazine, newspaper or website, you probably want to write features – which is the industry term for an article.

Of course, you don't have to freelance to write features and articles. You might work full-time as a features writer – just like we both did when we worked for magazines.

However, we find that if you already have a day job in another field and want to write features, you're likely to start off as a freelance writer rather than a full-time one.

The great thing about freelance writing is that the world is your oyster.

Got a passion for bonsai? Write an article about it.

Want to travel the world? Write travel articles!

Interested in the share market? Write articles where you can interview brokers.

Keen on meeting fellow Trekkies? Write an article about obsessed Star Trek fans.

The key skill of a freelance feature writer is to be able to research the topic at hand, interview relevant people and convey that information in a compelling article. Basically, it's a great chance to ask a bunch of questions to interesting people about topics that fascinate you!

Some freelance writers choose to specialise and write about a particular topic. So you might decide that you only want to write about small business. Or you want to focus on writing about the arts. Or you really just want to write about music. Or beer. Or dogs. Or home decor. Some of our graduates have chosen exactly those topics to channel their energies into. It's up to you!

It's a path that freelance writer Cat Rodie has navigated successfully. She never thought she'd become a writer. This limiting belief, coupled with her experience with dyslexia, meant she hadn't considered that writing could be a real career for her. But after completing a course at the Australian Writers' Centre, that all changed. And now, she's become one of the most prolific freelance writers in Australia, with her byline appearing in many of the country's top publications.

It's a profession that gives her the flexibility to dictate her own hours. "I get to work for myself, set my own hours, I can get on with work after my kids have gone to bed, or first thing in the morning if I get up before them. I can fit it around all the other responsibilities I have with them... taking them to school, their sports activities and playdates and everything else that comes with having young children. I was talking to a mum at a swimming lesson recently and she was telling me about this brilliant article she'd read that had really made her laugh. I said, 'Oh I think I wrote that,' and it felt so good."

The content writer

There's a lot of crossover and similarity between the world of freelance feature writing and content writing. Many freelance feature writers, who usually cut their teeth writing for magazines, newspapers and online publications, are adding content writing to what they offer because it brings another revenue stream to their overall income.

Content writing uses almost exactly the same principles as feature writing, but there are some subtle nuances you need to know about in order to succeed.

Before you launch into this space it's important to understand where this explosion in content writing has come from.

In the past, if you wanted to get published as a freelance writer, your main options were to be published by mainstream or trade publications. For example, *Real Living* (published by Bauer Media), *Daily Life* (Fairfax) or *Vogue Australia* (NewsLifeMedia).

However, an increasing number of companies are now becoming publishers.

Some have been publishers for a while. Think of Qantas and its inflight magazine, or a health fund like HCF posting out its magazine to letterboxes each month.

These companies have typically outsourced the writing and magazine production to mainstream publishers that have a department dedicated to serving corporate clients.

Other companies choose to do it in-house. They employ their own editors, designers and so on to produce the magazine.

Traditionally this been called custom publishing, but some companies now call it content – or content marketing.

It doesn't matter what the term is – that's just semantics. *It's content that's written to appear in a publication or online for a company or organisation.*

Specifically, content writing is the art of communicating without overt selling – and this often takes the form of providing helpful or entertaining information to your target audience.

The real explosion in content writing is online, and companies are now running their own online publications in the hope they'll attract eyeballs. For example, a health or pharmaceutical company may run an informational website on how to look after newborns.

The information is certainly useful, but the reality is that the information is being hosted on its own website, with its own subtle (or not so subtle) branding. The company wants to reach its target market with this information but also hopes its audience will eventually buy its products for newborns.

The same goes for a bank. It provides information about personal finance in the hope that consumers will one day do business with them.

Then there's the lawyer who provides information on the steps you need to take to get divorced in the hope you'll engage his or her services if you ever need that kind of advice.

The exact same principles apply for both regular feature articles for mainstream publications and content writing for companies and businesses. You still need a great hook, a strong angle and various subtopics in your story. In many cases, you also need to have expert opinions and case studies.

The main difference in writing content for companies and businesses is that there may be a different angle or emphasis in the story compared to the one you'd use for a mainstream publication.

Think about it logically. If you were writing a story about how hard it is for the average Australian to save up a deposit for a house, then in a regular feature article you might quote an expert from the Commonwealth Bank, a spokesperson from Westpac and some case studies of how people have saved up their deposits.

However, if you're writing content for the Commonwealth Bank website, you're not going to quote someone from Westpac, are you?

Or let's say you're writing an article on how to soothe eczema in babies. If you wrote it for a parenting magazine you'd interview an expert and you might mention the various products they recommended.

However, if you're writing content for the Procter & Gamble website, you may still quote the expert, but you're unlikely to mention products the expert recommends if they're made by Procter & Gamble's competitors.

If you want to delve into the world of content writing, we strongly recommend you improve your skills in feature writing first and then learn the subtle nuances you'll need to employ in content writing.

The blog and social media writer

Blogging is a particular form of writing that toes a line between intimate and commercial. It's something you can do for yourself – or be paid to do for others. A blog allows a writer to build a profile that can then be leveraged by companies (in sponsored content). Or companies will pay a writer with a large following for the eyeballs they can bring to the company's website.

Blogging essentially makes the writer publisher of their own work, and often goes hand-in-hand with creating social media content as the writer works to build an audience for that work. Both of these things create a suite of marketable skills that a writer can use to make a living from their words.

If this is an area of writing that interests you, dip your toes in with a personal blog or a blog about your area of expertise. Begin by reading other blogs, connecting with the blogging community and getting an idea of what others are doing to turn their passions into paid opportunities.

If nothing else, the discipline of writing regularly on a blog is great practice for life as a working writer!

The copywriter

Traditionally, a copywriter is someone who writes *words that sell*. That may include advertisements, brochures, websites, direct marketing communication and so on. Specifically, copywriting is about writing words designed to move someone to take action – and often that action is buying a product or service.

Ever seen *Mad Men*? It's the award-winning television series set in the world of advertising agencies in the 1950s and 1960s. This world was originally the domain of copywriters – those who wrote the words for the ads that Don Draper would so adeptly pitch to clients. He'd then celebrate the clients' acceptance of their new slogan by downing a scotch or two from the conveniently located decanter in his office.

Since then, as marketers find more ways to influence unsuspecting consumers, the field of copywriting has evolved to encompass all other words that sell – even down to the messages that shout at you from the petrol bowser encouraging you to buy a soft drink and a chocolate bar for a special price!

However, the idea of the copywriter has evolved again and many people use the term quite loosely these days.

As we've mentioned, technically a copywriter writes words that sell. But thanks to the explosion in content writing, many clients now ask their copywriters to also write their content. Why? Because it's just easier to deal with the same writer – one who already knows the business – than have to engage a new writer for the content.

What's the difference between copywriting and content writing? It's subtle, but think of it this way. If you're writing for a bank, a traditional copywriter would write the messages on the advertisements in magazines or posters about new home loans for millennials that are now available. However, a content writer is more likely to write an article on the bank's website on "how millennials can save for their first deposit". See the difference?

You don't *have* to do both copywriting and content writing. Some choose to offer both but you can choose to focus solely on copywriting or solely on content writing. Many writers do.

However, it's important to recognise that many clients often don't use the right term. They ask for a copywriter when they really want a content writer – and vice versa. Again, it's just semantics, but as long as you ask the right questions so you're clear on the outcome they want to achieve, you can then determine whether your skills fit the bill.

If you decide to work as a copywriter, you can write about a range of topics. Or you could also specialise. Donna Webeck completed the copywriting course at the Australian Writers' Centre and is now in demand as a copywriter in the real estate industry. It means she can combine her love of writing with her passion for houses.

Donna first dabbled in the world of freelance feature writing before deciding to focus on copywriting. "I did the Copywriting Essentials course," she says. "And that's when it sparked everything off and I thought, 'This is where I can make a business out of this sector, this particular genre of writing.'"

The technical writer

For something quite different, there are also technical writers who write to convey technical, scientific or industry-specific issues in plain, easily understandable English – like manuals on how to use software.

It takes a very ordered and systematic mind to be an effective technical writer. You often need to be able to talk to experts – such as software programmers, engineers, scientists, analysts and the like – and communicate what they mean in a layperson's terms.

It's also important to have empathy with the end user. You need to be able to put yourself in their shoes and write instructions in plain English and in a logical order.

Technical writers usually have some kind of experience in the industry they're working in and can come into these roles through sideways moves. For example, an IT programmer who might not be keen on programming anymore but enjoys writing can combine these skills and become a technical writer for Microsoft.

The scriptwriter

Whether you're writing scripts for television, movies, plays or commercials, a scriptwriter has a unique set of skills that are required for this very visual medium.

This kind of writing is also usually a lot more collaborative than other types of writing. Scriptwriters will often have to deal with producers, directors, script editors, studios and even actors.

There's a lot more to consider than just telling a story. Scriptwriters have to take into account the number of minutes a script can run for, what time it will screen on TV or the rating it will be given by the movie classification board (as this may influence the type of intimate scenes, the language or the level of violence included in the show).

They also have to take budget into account. After all, you can't write in too many explosion scenes if the production company simply can't afford them. Or you can't have a scene set in a crowded party if the studio doesn't have the budget for many extras!

PR and corporate communications writers

There are also writers who specialise in public relations or corporate communications. This means they mainly write documents like press releases, annual reports, CEO speeches, and other corporate communications materials. Most of this writing is often done by the in-house public relations staff, that is the consultants who deal with the clients on a day-to-day basis.

However, sometimes this material is outsourced to freelance specialist corporate communications writers. These people typically gain their skills as journalists – or within a PR consultancy – before branching into this area.

The reason for this is that an effective corporate communications writer is one who understands how to write press releases in the style and format similar to the articles that appear in magazines and newspapers.

What appeals to you?

As we've said, this list is by no means exhaustive, but it does cover some of the more popular types of writing. We find that most people either want to:

- write fiction with a view to possibly publishing a novel one day
- become freelance writers who write features, content or copywriting

If you want to write fiction, it's a long-term activity. You can't write a good book in a month and magically find a publisher straight away. It takes a bit longer than that!

However, you can learn the skills to become a freelance writer fairly quickly if you get the right instruction and advice. We've known many students who've done our course in freelance writing and have been able to find paid work almost immediately.

In fact, if you're interested in both fiction and freelance writing, you can do what some of our graduates do. Patrick, an architect who decided to transition into the world of writing, learnt the skills he needed to earn his income as a freelance feature writer – writing predominantly about aviation – and carved out a niche in this space. He also learnt the craft of writing children's books and penned his manuscripts in his spare time.

However, if you have no interest in writing fiction and just want to focus on freelance writing because you want to earn an income this way, that's fine too. Freelance writing suits people who need a bit of instant gratification! You'll see the outcome from writing an 800-word article a lot quicker than it would take to write an 80,000-word book.

Relatively speaking, it doesn't take long to write and research an article – and then see it published.

Alternatively, you might be happy to chip away at a manuscript of the epic fantasy that's playing out in your head while you're in your day job as a florist. For you, it's just a pleasure to write and you don't mind how long it takes you.

You can offer a portfolio of styles

Some people have a portfolio of styles they can offer. During a period in Valerie's freelance career, she wrote non-fiction books, freelanced regularly for *The Sydney Morning Herald*, wrote corporate communications documents for finance and IT companies and wrote celebrity profiles – all at the same time.

"I loved the variety," she says. "I loved the idea of interviewing a rock star one day and a CEO the next. Plus, writing corporate communications documents for major multinationals was very lucrative – and that took the pressure off if I wanted to spend a long time researching and working on a celebrity interview."

Similarly, Allison, who now focuses on children's fiction, began her writing life as a sub-editor who occasionally wrote features, dropping back to three days a week in that role so she could build a freelance writing portfolio. By the time her first child was born, she was working full-time as a freelance writer – doing features, corporate work, paid blogging and content creation – and had begun working on what became her first manuscript.

"I juggled freelance work, teaching writing, raising kids and slogging away at my fiction for years, with the paid work always coming first," Allison says. "Now that I'm a published children's author, the only thing that has changed is that I don't do as much freelance writing anymore, but I've added in a lot more work as a professional speaker, thanks to my books."

Follow your own path

Whatever path – or combination of paths – you take, the beauty of writing is that it's flexible, fun and creatively satisfying.

Once you decide what kind of writer you'd like to be, you just need to determine what skills you need in order to be good at it. And we're here to help you do that!

Just believe it can happen. Remember Rule number one? You need to believe that it's possible. And it is! We see people achieve their writing goals again and again. The common element among all of them is that they believe they can do it.

One of the biggest reasons people don't think it's possible to achieve their particular writing dreams is that they don't know what they need to do to make it happen. It can be pretty daunting when you have no clue what your pathway should be.

But don't worry, you don't have to have an entire pathway lit up in front of you showing every single step that's required before you get to your goal. Even though we're showing you a step-by-step plan towards your goals, sometimes it can be hard to see how you'll ever get to step five when you're only at step one.

Just focus on where you are at right now. And as you progress, the next step in your path will be illuminated – and you'll have the confidence and motivation to move forward with it.

CHAPTER 4
What skills do you need?

Let's say you've considered what kind of writing you want to pursue. And you've come up with a handful of writing styles you'd like to explore. Or maybe you're already singularly focused on one particular path.

Whatever your situation, the next step is to determine what kind of skills you really need in order to succeed.

The answer is different for everyone. If you want to write a picture book, you'll need to learn a completely different set of skills to someone who wants to write psychological thrillers.

If you want to be a content writer or copywriter, that requires a completely different set of skills compared to what you'd need to know as a writer of literary fiction.

So if you want to fast-track your success, you have to know exactly which skills you need to hone – and the best way to do that.

How do you determine this?

In some cases, the answer is very obvious. For example, if you want to improve your skills in writing, chances are there's a course for your needs at the Australian Writers' Centre, available online or on campus. Courses cover writing novels, short stories, picture books, memoir, freelance writing, copywriting, content, business writing, travel writing and so on. Some other writers centres also offer excellent courses. Some do not.

Always make sure that whatever course you enrol in has a good reputation and is taught by an industry expert who's also an encouraging and inspiring teacher. How do you determine that? Of course, you can rely on testimonials and reviews, but word-of-mouth is also a great resource. Ask for an opinion from someone who's already done the course so you can get a first-hand account of what it was like.

Courses – whether or not the Australian Writers' Centre offers them – are the ideal place to start when you're looking to improve your skills.

As we've already mentioned, they help you experience different types of writing in a safe environment. And they give you the room to experiment and discover whether you're passionate about this type of writing.

'But I can't do a course!'

If you're already a course junkie, fantastic. We salute you – we'll see you in a course soon!

However, we know that some of you aren't fond of the idea of doing a course. Or perhaps it feels too hard.

I live too far away.

Even if there is an online course, I prefer the classroom environment but I'm not near one.

I'm secretly antisocial and don't want to be with people.

I'm scared about what the teacher will say if they read my work.

I don't have the time.

The kids are too demanding and I won't have time to do any assignments.

I prefer to learn by myself through YouTube videos.

I'm too busy at work right now.

I have to wait till the kids grow up.

I write all day at work, I can't be creative in my spare time so I won't be able to appreciate the course.

My dog ate my homework.

Heard these before?

You know what they are? They're excuses!

Sure, sometimes we really are slammed with work. And sometimes the kids do pull us in too many directions. But if you really want to explore the world of writing, you need to do something to push yourself in the right direction.

If your schedule won't allow you to join a course with a set start date, we've created online self-paced courses at the AWC just so people can fit them into their own busy lifestyles. No specific times, no pressure to hang out with other people.

But we sometimes hear the same excuses! Only *you* truly know whether you're making a valid excuse or if you're simply procrastinating.

If it's the former, we understand how you feel. We've been there! Life will calm down soon and we know you'll be ready.

If it's the latter, you know you'll be saying the same thing in two years' time. But we want to encourage you to break out of that cycle of excuses – and take action.

When you procrastinate too much, you end up being overwhelmed with guilt. And that turns into frustration. It's a unique kind of guilt, the kind you feel because you know you're just short-changing yourself. And when you keep doing that, you end up secretly angry that you're not putting yourself first.

If you keep making excuses, it becomes so frustrating that you may end up trying to convince yourself you "never really wanted to become a writer in the first place". Don't let yourself cop out like this. Give yourself a chance to explore a new world of creativity. You have nothing to lose, and everything to gain.

Time for a coffee

In addition to learning through courses or workshops, a great way to learn about the industry and the skills you need to acquire is to talk to people who are already doing what you hope to do one day.

We're big fans of having coffee with people. Of course, you don't have to drink coffee. You can order a soy chai, a kombucha or even a glass of wine. Whatever takes your fancy!

This isn't because we're lobbyists for the beverage industry. "Having coffee" is just another way to describe the "information interview". And these interviews are incredibly useful.

What is an information interview? It's simply a chat with someone to find out how they got into their line of work.

If you come across someone who works as a writer in a field you find interesting, make sure you ask for their business card. Or ask if it's okay for you to connect with them on LinkedIn.

Or perhaps you have a friend who can put you in touch with their neighbour who happens to be a scriptwriter. Or the copywriter they use for their business.

Okay, we can hear you say: "What if I haven't made any contacts with any appropriate people?" The answer is easy – just make some. We know that sounds simple – but that's because it is. Just think about what would be the most logical way to contact them.

Let's say you've dreamt of being a novelist, contact the publisher of your favourite ones. The publisher will be listed in the front of the author's book. These days, many authors also have their own website and many publish their email addresses. Or you can often meet them at writers' festivals and at workshops and courses they teach.

If you want to write columns in newspapers, contact established columnists via the newspaper they write for. Often they display their Twitter handles or email addresses on their columns – or these can easily be found on the newspaper's website.

Don't be shy about contacting people. They may not all answer – but some of them might. All it takes is a well-crafted sincere email and perhaps a follow-up phone call or email.

You might feel slightly intimidated calling or emailing these people out of the blue. But just remind yourself that they're normal people doing a regular job just like you. Really, there isn't anything to be intimidated about.

Many years ago, when Valerie was starting out in her writing career, she emailed TV personality Tony Squires for advice. At the time he wrote a popular column about television every week in *The Sydney Morning Herald*, and Valerie used to love it – because she's obsessed with TV!

"It took him weeks to respond, but he did," says Valerie. "And he did so in a very lengthy, motivating and inspirational email. At the time, I was an aspiring writer so it encouraged me no end."

If you want to be a scriptwriter, contact the script editors or writers on TV shows you admire. Again, many years ago, Valerie contacted the script department of a popular Australian cop show.

"I had no experience in scriptwriting but, when I contacted the head of the script department, I made it very clear that I was sincere and willing to learn about the industry and serious about exploring it for a possible career change," she recalls.

"The script department allowed me to be a fly on the wall and work with them for a whole week! It was a tremendous opportunity to see the inner workings of a TV show's script production process. And an opportunity not many people get – *simply because they don't ask.*"

Valerie notes that she was not in Year 9 looking for work experience. "I was old enough to have a kid in Year 9 at the time! It's never too late to change careers, and you're never too old to ask for advice.

"In the end, I decided that, while the scriptwriting process was fascinating, I wanted to concentrate on other types of writing. That was just my personal preference. But my time exploring scriptwriting wasn't wasted because it means I can say I gave it a go and I figured out it wasn't for me.

"I wouldn't always be wondering, 'What if?' It also helped to steer me into the kind of writing I do now – which I love."

The information interview is so effective because you're merely asking someone for information and advice. And guess what? People love to talk about themselves!

When you approach people, make it clear you're not after

anything except for information and advice. People are going to be more responsive than if you're hoping for something more – like a job or part-time work. If they think you're ultimately looking for a job, they're not as likely to meet up with you unless a position is actually available.

Need help? Try something like this when you call or email:

My name is Mary Jones. I'm a keen reader of your column/novels/ scripts/articles/writing and would really value your advice about how to get into journalism/publishing/scriptwriting etc. I hope to be in a role like yours one day. I'm currently working as a dental technician, but I've done a couple of short writing courses and I've really enjoyed them.

If you have a spare 10 minutes, I'd appreciate the chance to conduct an information interview with you – just so I can ask you some questions about the industry and hear your advice on what you think I could do to help my career. I'm happy to meet with you in your office or talk on the phone if that's more convenient.

It's just a few simple sentences, but it's flattering, non-threatening and straight to the point.

We know countless people who have made valuable contacts as a result of 10-minute information interviews. And many of them have eventually scored part-time, full-time or freelance roles as a result of making contact with the organisation, even though getting a job wasn't the primary aim of the interview. Their brief chat paid off big time.

Finding mentors or role models

Some of the people you speak to in your information interviews may end up being your mentors or role models. Or you may find mentors through another avenue.

Having a mentor is a wonderful way to fast-track your progress. At best, they may be able to introduce you to opportunities that can help you on your journey to becoming a writer. You shouldn't necessarily expect or feel entitled to that when you enter into a mentoring relationship, but it's a great bonus if it does happen.

Valerie is now a big believer in the power of having a mentor, but it's a lesson she didn't learn until later in her life. "Obviously, I understood what a mentor was when I was younger. But I never sought one out," she says. "And I wish I had. I sometimes wonder whether it had something to do with being an only child and learning to be self-sufficient for so long. It never occurred to me to ask people for advice, I always thought I had to figure it all out by myself.

"Eventually, at the tender age of 38, I finally found a mentor. Even then, I wasn't looking for one. He just took it upon himself to contact me regularly and began mentoring me. I guess he saw that he could make a difference in my career progression.

"It was transformative. He helped me think a lot bigger and, after all those years trying to figure out everything on my own, I finally realised how beneficial it was to have guidance from someone who's already walked the path you want to go down. It made me realise how much I'd been missing out on.

"If there was one thing in my life I wish I'd done differently, it would be to seek out the right mentors much earlier."

How to find the right mentor

Let us state from the outset that finding a mentor is a bit like dating. Sometimes you need to kiss a few frogs before you find "The One". But unlike dating, there's a lot less angst and emotional trauma involved!

If a certain mentor doesn't work out, don't chuck a hissy fit and assume that mentoring is not for you. Just try others until you find the one best suited to your needs. It's the same as any other service-based relationship, whether you're trying out a physiotherapist, dentist, cleaner or hairdresser. If you're not enamoured with them, that's fine. Just move on until you find the right one.

Paid and unpaid mentoring relationships

There are people who offer paid mentorships and those who'll enter into a more informal unpaid mentoring relationship.

Paid mentors: You can pay mentors who will typically give you feedback on technical aspects of your writing. They may help you craft pitches to editors, agents or publishers.

You have a professional relationship with these mentors, and it's likely they'll have clear deliverables on the service they'll provide based on what you're paying them. We're not going to spend a lot of time on this category, because it's a fairly straightforward transactional relationship. You just need to determine whether what they offer is right for you – and whether you're willing to pay for it.

However, there are also more informal unpaid mentoring relationships. What do they look like and how do you find one?

Informal unpaid mentors: These mentors typically don't advertise this as a service. They enter into informal mentoring relationships usually because they happen to like the mentoree and want to see them succeed. They're effectively participating for altruistic reasons.

How do you get one of these mentors? After all, there's no such directory of well-meaning people! Remember how we think that "having coffee" is a great approach? This is often the first step to finding a great mentor.

The best way to find a mentor is actually not to ask them to mentor you at your first meeting. Imagine going to a date with someone who then proposes marriage before you've even had dessert. You'd run a mile!

Plus there are very few people who will commit to an unpaid mentoring relationship with someone they barely know.

Instead, you do the dance. Have your coffee meeting. During your chat, feel free to ask their advice on your particular circumstances. Don't ask them to introduce you to anyone or open any doors for you. Wait until they offer to do this.

If you click, ask them if they'd mind if you could have another coffee in a few months' time, after you've had a chance to act on their valuable advice and have figured out what your next step might be.

If you do this a few times, you've effectively entered into an informal mentoring relationship. Just let it evolve naturally over time.

It's a two-way street

The biggest mistake we see people make is when they just take, take and then take some more.

If you're paying your mentor, that's fine. There's a clear transaction. But if you're not paying your mentor, remember that it's a two-way street.

This means that if you can return the favour in any way, do so. Perhaps your mentor may not need any of your services, but the gesture of buying them coffee, lunch, flowers or sending them a small but thoughtful gift can go a long way towards showing you appreciate them. And they're more likely to genuinely consider you as a mentoree instead of just a user.

When you're talking to a mentor, here are some useful points of discussion:

- How did you get your break into the industry?
- What's the best thing about what you do?
- What's the most challenging thing about what you do?
- If you had your time again, what would you do differently?
- I'd like to do [fill in whatever writing goal you have]. What steps do you think I should take to get there?
- What skills do you think I should improve in order to reach my goal?
- What's the biggest mistake that people in my position make when pursuing this goal?
- Are there any organisations I should avoid? Why?
- Is there anyone you think I should talk to who might be able to offer me some advice in this area?

You'll find that these talking points will often open up areas of discussion and reveal new writing avenues you hadn't previously considered.

Talk to 'leading learners'

When you're looking for mentors it can be easy to think you have to talk to the CEO of a publishing house, or a successful author, or a renowned magazine writer. And if you *can* talk to these people, go right ahead.

However, don't forget that it's equally useful to talk to those who are just a little bit ahead of you, those who were in your position not that long ago.

We call these people "leading learners". They're still learning about the world of writing, but they've been delving into this world just a little bit longer than you have.

These people are often much more accessible than someone who's already a veteran of the industry. And it's great to hear from someone who's only a few steps ahead of where you are now.

They can give you advice on courses, writing communities, festivals they've attended – and share what they got out of these activities. They can also give you an insight into how they improved their writing skills and the techniques they've used to progress in their journey.

And that brings us to another valuable – and fun – aspect of your path to becoming a writer. Finding your tribe.

CHAPTER 5
Finding your tribe

Writing is a very solitary activity. And if you're an introvert, that's probably one thing you love about it! In fact, both of us secretly relish the fact that we can hang out at home, wear no makeup, don our trakkies and take great pleasure in the fact that we don't have to see another human being all day.

However, if you want to become a writer – if you want to succeed at anything – you need the support of other people.

We love the saying made famous by entrepreneur Jim Rohn: "You are the average of the five people you spend most time with."

It makes sense, right? If you're always around negative people, it's easy for that negativity to rub off on you. If you're around positive people, you're more likely to have a positive outlook.

It's not rocket science. And yet sometimes we choose to fly in the face of this logic when we decide who to spend our time with.

Seek out people who are going to lift you higher. If you want to become a writer, look for ways you can spend more time with other writers – whether that's in person or online. The wonderful thing about today's hyperconnected age is that you don't have to live in a big city to access wonderful online networks where you can connect with other writers. As a start, just look at the proliferation of Facebook groups for writers.

Sure, it's always better to be able to connect with someone in real life. But if you live a zillion kilometres away from these opportunities, that's no excuse these days. Just go online!

Valerie sometimes talks about how a group of 10-year-olds shaped her future. She explains: "Kylie. Philippa. Adam. David. John. Juanita. Gina. Nerida. Troy. Steven. Michelle. Brooke. Amanda. Karin… I can tell you the names of almost every student in my Year 5 class with Mr Timmermann at Sutherland Primary School," she says.

"I didn't realise it back then, but my experiences with this class later became the foundation for some of my guiding principles in life."

You need to find *your* tribe. That tribe needs to consist of people who inspire you to be better, do better, tap into your potential and discover more about yourself.

"Of course, at the tender age of 10, I didn't think these guys were my tribe," says Valerie. "They were simply Kylie, my bestie from down the road. Or Adam who loved *The Goon Show* and came to the school dance dressed as Adam Ant. Or David with the squeaky voice. Or Philippa who was mad about sport.

"But thanks to our teacher Mr Timmermann, we were all encouraged to learn. He motivated us to pursue our interests and gently pushed us to discover more about the world around us. And we all did.

"We'd see a picture of a thatched hut and Mr Timmermann would get us to build one. We'd talk about stars in the sky and the next thing we knew we were on an excursion to the observatory. We'd then learn about gravity and build a cardboard version of a space shuttle.

"We'd read a novel with a scene about how a car broke down and soon we were researching and drawing the inner workings of a carburettor. He helped us understand that we could learn about – and do – *anything we wanted to*. Somehow, he created an environment where we all wanted to learn and excel at what we did."

At the time, Valerie had no idea what a gift this experience was. "It taught me what it was like when you were surrounded by other motivated and like-minded kids who were curious and loved the process of discovery."

That's the magic about being in a community. And it was the real-life manifestation of Jim Rohn's quote: "You are the average of the five people you spend most time with."

Fill your world with people who inspire you. They aren't always obvious. They come in all shapes, races and ages, but one thing they have in common is that they climb tall mountains. And, from there, they see even taller mountains still left to climb. They say yes to challenges – and they believe anything is possible.

That means you need to be really honest with yourself. Who are you spending your time with? Are they naysayers who think that your dreams of becoming a writer are pie in the sky? Do they understand when you say you need to write on Sunday afternoon? Or do they shame you into going to the pub when you'd rather be tapping out the story that's been busting to get out of your head?

We're not suggesting you ditch your current friends and only make friends with successful people. We're just saying that you need the right environment and the right support if you need encouragement or a boost to your self-belief. Because when you see others like you achieving, you'll start to believe you can do it too.

Where can you find your tribe or community? There's no set answer to this, because everyone wants different things. But here are some ideas to get you started.

Courses

If you're at the start of your journey, a great place to connect with like-minded people is through courses. If you're doing the same course, you already have a common interest.

Sure, you're not going to click with everyone on your course, but that regular dose of conversation with other aspiring writers can be a great motivation if you're surrounded by non-writerly types the rest of your day.

Alumni groups

If you're a graduate of the Australian Writers' Centre, you'll know there are Facebook groups for graduates that are designed to create and nurture relationships among people who've done the same course. It's been incredible to see many close friendships emerge from these online groups – often between people who live nowhere near each other.

They're a great way to discover news about the industry, hear about writing opportunities and to share resources. The beauty is that everyone in the group has done the same course so there's an assumed base level of knowledge.

Writer Lisa Schofield believes these communities are invaluable. When Lisa worked in banking, she never dreamt she'd one day become a freelance journalist and corporate writer. But she's now been successfully published in countless magazines and newspapers – and is in demand as a writer contracting to the corporate world she was once a part of.

"Before I did the Freelance Writing course at the Australian Writers' Centre, I'd never have imagined myself being in this situation," Lisa says. "I've gone up a level of professionalism in my writing and that wouldn't have been possible without doing the course.

"I learnt all the elements I needed to be able to write. Before, I didn't know how to write – or how to start. I didn't know the technical aspects of writing, and I felt like I needed to go somewhere with experts who knew how to do it and to train myself up – just like you'd train yourself in any job. I knew I had the passion, I knew I had the ability – but I didn't know how to do it.

"One of the other benefits is that I've met other writers and have become part of a community. That community is very strong. It's precious to us. We all look after and nurture each other, and that gives us the confidence to take risks and do braver things. I work alone in my office, but I feel like I'm not alone because I have so many online friends – and real friends – that I've met through the Australian Writers' Centre course."

Other online groups

There are online groups for everything! We even have one for our podcast listeners on Facebook. Just search for "So you want to be a writer podcast community" and request to join.

The best way to find the right one for you is to get a recommendation. If your pal loves a particular online group for writers, give it a go. In the absence of a recommendation, just search, join up and sample what they have to offer. These groups are usually free, so you have nothing to lose.

The key is to give it some time. Don't just join for a week and then opt out if you don't suddenly score a book deal during your short stay there. Contribute, ask questions and share your experiences with other people when you can. Always make sure you read any group protocols or rules and follow them.

Groups of this nature usually only succeed when there are some strong leaders who encourage conversation, share ideas and aren't afraid to set the tone of the group. You'll soon find out whether it's a group that's going to work for you.

Critique or writing groups

Many aspiring and established novelists swear by their critique groups, which are also known as writing groups. These are small groups of two to eight people who read each other's manuscripts and provide feedback on what works and what doesn't.

There's sometimes a bit of wine and socialising thrown in as well, but the main purpose of the group is to get feedback on your writing from someone who's not your mother. Someone who will truly analyse what your characters are doing and give you some tough love about an unwieldy scene so you can improve on it in your next draft.

Author Margaret Morgan found her critique group when she completed a novel writing course at the Australian Writers' Centre.

"The best aspect of the course was learning how to critique

and prepare a structural edit," she says. "By applying those skills to each other's manuscripts, we learnt how to use them to improve our own work.

"Also, meeting up with like-minded aspiring novelists was invaluable. I still meet regularly with the writing group we formed after the course ended."

This approach obviously worked! The result was Margaret's debut novel, *The Second Cure*, which is now being turned into a television series.

Writers' conferences

These are a wonderful way to network and discover people in your industry. Writers' conferences are typically held by industry bodies and associations. They are usually about the exchange of relevant information helpful to members and attendees. There is a combination of professional development and career-related advice as well as sessions about craft and trends.

If you want to know which ones to attend so you can connect with more people in your field, it's pretty simple. One easy way to determine who the players are in your industry is to look at the list of speakers at a conference. If they're going to be on stage, chances are they have something interesting to say.

Try to chat to them after their sessions, mention something you found interesting and ask if it would be okay if you contacted them for advice in the future. They could be one of your "coffees" or information interviews.

Another tip is to make sure you go to morning tea, lunch and afternoon tea during the conference. It's not that we're policing your nutritional intake, but when it comes to a busy conference where you're surrounded by a bunch of people you don't know it can be *very* tempting to retreat to your hotel room, or go and sit in a café around the corner so you don't have to talk to anyone.

Resist this! We know – you're an introvert and you'd rather be by yourself. You can be by yourself later that night when the conference is over. That's because some of the best connections you'll ever make will be made in the lobby as you balance your Earl Grey tea in one hand and a scone in another, while trying to read the name tag of the person who's just started talking to you.

Valerie says, "I know people who'll turn up to conferences without paying for a ticket and just hang out in the lobby because they know that's where they'll make their most valuable connections."

We don't actually suggest you freeload in this way. But we *do* believe that conferences are a wonderful opportunity to really get an insight into the industry. And one of the best things about them is that everyone you'd want to know is literally under one roof.

To figure out which conferences to go to, Google is your friend. If you're into romance writing, Google "Romance writers' conference". If you like writing for children, Google "children's writing conference". If you like crime writing… you get the idea!

Going to conferences pays off. Take children's book author Shelly Unwin, who landed a wonderful agent – and subsequently multiple publishing contracts – at a writers' conference. Shelly had completed a few courses at the Australian Writers' Centre, including the course Writing Picture Books, and had begun networking at industry conferences.

Shelly says, "I'd spent three years attending as many writing conferences and networking events with editors as possible, and having one-on-one consultations to get feedback on my works in progress.

"As part of this process, I attended a literary speed-pitching session which is run like a speed-dating session! That's where I met my lovely agent, Alex Adsett. On that day I was pitching my young adult novel, and I'd done such a bad job with the first editor I pitched to that I thought, 'I really need to give this another go.' Alex was there and, when I pitched it to her, she was so lovely and encouraging.

"Before the event, I'd read what Alex was looking for – and she wasn't looking for picture books. But after my YA pitch I said, 'I don't suppose you'd be interested in hearing my pitch for my picture books, would you?' She replied, 'Yeah, tell me.' So I pitched my *You're One!* series to her and she seemed very enthusiastic.

"Very soon after the conference, she agreed to represent me. There were a couple of publishing houses interested and the series went to a small auction which Alex negotiated."

Shelly's debut series of picture books, the *You're One!* series, has become hugely popular in Australia and has also been sold into North America. Shelly's now published seven picture books, including *Blast Off!* and *There's a Baddie Running Through this Book!*.

Writers' festivals

There are writers' festivals all around Australia and they're incredible fun. They're a wonderful way to hear your favourite authors, get your books signed and absorb all things literary for a few days. However, the term "writers' festival" can be a bit misleading. Sure, there are heaps of writers at these festivals, but the sessions typically cater to readers.

There are panels on the ideas and themes portrayed in certain books. There are sessions dedicated to iconic or villainous characters depicted in famous novels. There are one-on-one conversations with authors. And there are book launches and parties to boot.

There are also a handful of workshops or panels directed at aspiring writers, which can be very useful. However, if you're going to a major festival, the sheer size of it makes networking difficult. The Sydney Writers' Festival has more than 300 events and attracts up to 100,000 people. That's a lot!

Don't get us wrong. We think you should still go. We certainly go to them, and we have a ball! But if you want the chance to make deeper connections with people in the industry, a writers' *conference* can be more conducive to doing that simply because it's smaller. Of course, one way to foster deeper connections at a writers' festival is to volunteer. That way, you get behind the scenes and have the opportunity to meet more people.

Hashtags

A more informal and organic way to connect with your tribe is to follow certain hashtags on social media. For example, #amwriting and #writingcommunity are often posted by budding and established authors when they post about writing their manuscript. They might be struggling with a plot point, or cheering the fact they've reached a certain word count.

When you follow and interact with others who are using those hashtags you're participating in a conversation with like-minded writers. It's a way to support each other and connect with others who are going through the same thing you are.

Of course, that doesn't mean you'll suddenly become best

friends and get invited to each other's weddings. But, over time, you'll end up forming deeper bonds with some of those people. We've both fostered many friendships which have originated on Twitter in this way.

Valerie initiated her last book deal with a publisher on Twitter. Similarly, Australian Writers' Centre alumna Jenna Guillaume, author of *What I Like About Me*, met her agent on Twitter, as did multi-published author and columnist Kerri Sackville.

CHAPTER 6
Where to find ideas

If you were to ask a roomful of published authors to nominate the question they're most often asked, there'd be one overwhelming response:

"Where do you get your ideas?"

This would apply whether they write children's fiction, adult fiction, non-fiction, fantasy, crime, romance, horror, picture books or any other kind of published work you can think of.

It's such a simple question, and yet one of the most difficult to answer in a succinct way.

The fact is that ideas are all around us, but they're rarely a one-off, lightning-bolt-from-the-blue event. It does happen that way, sure, but not very often.

The reality is that published authors are not superconductors of ideas. They're not magnets, attracting the best concepts like magic. They don't have ideas falling on their heads from above.

But they're observant.

They listen.

They watch closely.

They follow their passions, no matter how strange and quirky they may be.

They've trained their brains to ruminate and untangle and draw threads together.

As the American novelist Orson Scott Card once said, "Everybody walks past a thousand story ideas every day. The good writers are the ones who see five or six of them. Most people don't see any."

So how does it work?

Allison will tell you that her ideas are always based on a feeling and a question.

For instance, the entire concept for *The Mapmaker Chronicles* series – four books, 220,000 words – came from two conversations she had with her son, who was then nine years old. "How far does space go?" he asked her one night as they stood under the stars, staring out into the night.

"Nobody knows," she answered, holding his hand. Her mind whirled with that strange feeling of complete insignificance that the size of the universe evokes, and the overwhelming question of where the edges might be and what might await there.

The next night, he asked her a much more straightforward question: "How did they map the world?"

"Well," Allison replied, drawing on many years' interest in exploration and antique maps. "They had to go. They had to get into their ships and sail off onto endless oceans, not knowing what was out there and fairly certain they might never see their homes and families again."

In a moment of inspiration, she added, "They'd have felt the same way we felt when we stared out into space last night – they didn't know where the edges were."

In that moment, Allison knew she had a great idea for a story. A race to map the world – and a boy, her reluctant hero Quinn, who really didn't want to go. All based on a feeling and a question.

Her *Ateban Cipher* novels also came together based on a feeling and a question. An article in the newspaper about the mysterious Voynich Manuscript had Allison asking, "Why would you write a book that no-one can read?"

And the feeling? It came from Allison's passion for illuminated manuscripts – and from her overwhelming desire to possess *The Book of Kells* when she saw it on display at Dublin's Trinity College a decade earlier.

"I wanted it for myself," Allison recalls. "I wanted to reach through the alarms and the glass and just take it home with me."

While she managed to restrain herself from actually stealing the manuscript, that feeling never left her. And it was that sense of desire that partially drove the story in her *Ateban Cipher* series.

How does this help you?

If you listen to the writer-in-residence interviews in our *So You Want To Be A Writer* podcast, you'll hear that nearly every author has had a similar experience to Allison's. They've had an idea for a story that came together from two or three different sources.

It came from an overheard conversation, a snippet in a newspaper, a strange fascination with a quirky subject, a lightbulb moment when all of those pieces fell into place.

It's not just novelists and authors who experience this. Freelance writers, in particular, need to get very good at listening in to the conversations around them to find topical subjects for features, or scanning the headlines early in order to get in first with pitches for response articles or online features.

As with any skill, finding story ideas becomes easier the more you immerse yourself in the practice and open yourself up to different things to try.

Sometimes the story idea comes from a daily writing practice – the ability to sit down each morning and just write whatever's on your mind.

Sometimes it comes from a character, a little voice that pops up in your mind and won't go away.

Sometimes it's a "goodness me!" moment when you're watching a documentary about trains or canyons or whales or whatever the subject might be.

It might be your grandmother's story of moving to a new country. Or your aunt's story about setting up an orphanage overseas.

It might be that you absolutely love reading fantasy or crime or romance stories and you set out to write one of your own, drawing indirectly on every book you've ever read to create your own worlds.

Or it might be that you need a little help to recognise the wonderful ideas that are hanging about you right now, screaming for attention.

If any of those apply you, try these four tips to get you started.

Get a notebook

It's nice to think you'll recognise every genius idea you have and remember it, but you won't. You need to write it down. Even if it's half a snippet of conversation, or a news headline, or a fabulous fact about bee keeping, record it somewhere.

Every author has their own methods for keeping track of ideas – whether it be an actual notebook, a device of some kind, dictation (this works really well if you're in the car, and there are many apps to help), or rushing to their computer the minute they walk in the door.

Don't rely on your memory. Write down that idea. Yes, even if it comes to you in the middle of the night.

See the end of this chapter for 10 exercises to help you fill your notebook.

Research your quirks

New writers are often told to write what they know. That means they'll often begin with their own lives, which is fine, and sometimes you need to do this to get the "growing up in the 1990s almost-memoir" out of your brain. We have nothing against the "growing up in the 1990s almost-memoir", but it's important to recognise that what you know is not necessarily all about *you*.

Instead, look at what interests you. Maps and illuminated manuscripts worked well for Allison, but what's your quirky passion? Is it dogs? World War Two? The inner life of pandas? The art of botanical illustration? The secret story of tulips? All of these things have story potential. And the more you know, the more you have to work with – the more insight you have into that one, tiny thing that will kick off an epic narrative.

Turn off your devices

We can't emphasise enough the importance of tuning in to the world to glean ideas. If you're on your phone constantly, you're not listening to the conversations around you. You're not watching the interaction of the people on the street, feeling the hustle and bustle, taking in the quiet. You're not noticing what it feels like to sit on an empty beach, or in a noisy waiting room. In short, you're dulling your story antennae. Make a conscious decision to leave the device at home, or in your bag or pocket, at least once or twice a week.

Start a conversation

Allison's children will tell you that she's the world's most embarrassing "queue chatter". If there's a line to wait in, she'll always end up having a chat to the person standing next to her. Allison will tell you that this is just because she has a friendly face, but the truth is that the conversations begin because she's open to them. And she's open to them because you simply never know where the next story idea will come from.

Not only that, but every conversation you have adds to your "dialogue bank". So, in a non-creepy way, Allison is subconsciously taking note of the language that the elderly lady uses when she talks about the heat of the day. Or the body language of the middle-aged man who told her (completely unsolicited) about how he'd just been to the dentist and had an entirely new set of teeth – he was so incredibly happy to be able to smile again that he couldn't stop.

These sound like small things, but you never know where a little chat might take you, and any realistic detail you can add to a character will only strengthen your story.

Every person you meet has a story, and you never know what might kickstart your own. That's because most books are not the result of a single idea, but a drawing together of many.

Are you ignoring your best ideas?

The funny thing about great ideas is that they're often scary. Allison, for instance, never imagined she'd be an author of children's books, let alone children's series fiction.

"When I began writing fiction seriously in my late twenties, I took it all very seriously," Allison says. "I was working as a features writer at a major women's magazine and I approached my fiction in much the same way as I'd approach an article. I looked around to see where my market might be and I decided I'd write to target them."

Allison began writing romance novels, because they made sense to her. There were definite market segments, she'd worked hard on developing a commercial voice for magazine publishing, and she'd read, as she puts it, "shedloads of romance novels" in her late teens. How hard could it be?

As it turned out, it was a lot harder than she thought. "I really struggled to stay within the set word counts," Allison says. "I either tried to stuff too much into the story and the romance disappeared into a series of themes, or I concentrated on the romance to the point where my couple was breaking up over breakfast and back together by morning tea."

Aside from leaving Allison with a lasting respect for romance authors, the experience of writing two (unpublished) manuscripts in this area did have one great benefit.

"I wasn't wrong about the voice," Allison says. "It was enough to win me a mentor in a competition, and they gave me some great advice about 'going bigger' with my stories. I decided to try writing commercial women's fiction."

Another two full-length manuscripts later (180,000-plus words), Allison had been contracted to a publisher for one book, which unfortunately didn't quite get over the line. She was redrafting another when she had an idea.

Remember those two conversations Allison had with her son about space, maps and explorers? Well, that idea left her with a strange, tingling feeling – which she promptly ignored.

"I'd never written for children before," she says. "I had, of course, read hundreds of children's books, of all shapes and sizes, for all ages and stages, for myself and with my boys. I knew exactly the kind of story we love to read around here, with good guys and bad guys, a journey, a mystery and a sense of humour. Grand adventure stories that sweep you away from your safe, cosy bed and take you into other worlds. But writing one…"

Not having the faintest idea where to begin with the "tingly" idea, Allison tried to put it out of her mind and got on with writing her commercial women's fiction novel. The idea continued to nag at her, that race to map the world, but Allison was busy pursuing other goals and, frankly, just wasn't sure what to do with it.

That was until she had a conversation with her agent. "We were discussing what my next project might be. I was looking at a non-fiction book, and I also had an idea for another novel. Then, just as we were saying our goodbyes, she asked, 'I don't suppose you've got a middle-grade idea, do you? I'm being asked for manuscripts.'"

Allison admitted she'd had a "random idea about maps". That

conversation led to a manuscript, then a series synopsis, then a publishing contract.

"It was the wildest ride of my writing career," Allison says. "Writing *The Mapmaker Chronicles: Race to the End of the World* was the most fun I've ever had sitting at my desk. I *love* writing for children, and I might never have discovered that if I'd continued to ignore that crazy idea just because I'd never done it before."

Allison says she learnt three main lessons from this publishing adventure:

- Sometimes we don't choose the ideas – the ideas choose us.
- Embrace the big questions – you never know where they'll lead you.
- Never ignore that little tingle, even if you haven't tried something before and haven't the faintest notion of where to begin.

Start paying attention

Why might you ignore that little tingle? There are three main reasons.

1. You're trying to write 'what you know'

When you start out with writing, your first efforts are often semi-autobiographical, if not outright autobiographical. Or you'll begin, as Allison did, writing something you enjoy reading, or in a genre you think you understand well. We think this is often the case because it seems easier. (As Allison discovered, however, this is not necessarily the case…)

Admittedly, tackling a sweeping historical saga that draws on a lot of detailed research might be overwhelming for your first manuscript, so beginning with what you know is a great way to learn how you write a book. But this won't necessarily be your first published novel.

Write what you know, learn how you write a book, then give in to the nagging voice of that "best idea".

2. You're trying to be a certain kind of writer

If you have set ideas about the kind of writer you want to be, it's easy to overlook a really great idea simply because it doesn't fit your picture. There was no way a race to map the world was going to fit in a contemporary women's fiction manuscript, so Allison found it easy (at first!) to set it aside.

But if an idea continues to niggle at you and to demand attention, don't ignore it. Instead, consider whether or not you're willing to take a leap of faith to see if, in fact, you're simply a different writer than you thought you were.

Freelance writers should think about this too. You might stumble across a great idea for a news story, but try to ignore it because it seems too hard or something that more experienced journalists might need to do. But if it's an idea that seems important, and it's presented itself to you, what makes you think you're not the best person for the job?

Equip yourself with the skills you need – or perhaps approach a more experienced journalist to work with you on the story – and then pursue it.

3. You have no idea where to start

This one is easy to fix. If you have an idea full of romance but you've been busy writing hardboiled thrillers, learn how to write romance. Do a course. Read every romance novel you can get your hands on. Join an association of romance authors. Do what you can to further your knowledge before you discard your idea entirely.

The same goes for children's fiction, young adult fiction, picture books, fantasy, adventure, literary fiction – in fact, any kind of story you'd care to name. Talent will take you so far in the writing world, but learning your craft and applying those lessons to each and every manuscript, will take you so much further.

If you don't know how to write the story that's calling out to you, learn.

10 exercises to help you find your best ideas

You know us, we're never going to tell you that ideas are all around you and then not give your practical tips to help you corral those ideas. So get out your notebook and try at least five of these exercises to get you started.

1. **Go for a walk.** When you get home, write down the one thing that you most remember from the walk.

2. **Eavesdrop.** Do this in the nicest possible way – no glasses against closed doors! Next time you're sitting by yourself on a train, bus, in a restaurant, in a waiting room, in the park, (insert destination of choice), tune in to a conversation nearby for five minutes. Don't write anything down at this point – seriously, someone will call the police if you start transcribing their chat. When you get home, or to work, or wherever you're going, write down a few lines of the conversation in dialogue form, creating characterisation as you do so.

3. **Describe.** Write a paragraph describing a place you go to every day. Make it as interesting as possible for someone who's never been there. How much detail can you put into your paragraph? Often the places we're most familiar with are the hardest to describe.

4. **Watch.** Choose a documentary on a subject you know nothing about, and watch it from start to finish. Afterwards, write a short paragraph about the single most interesting detail you learnt from the documentary.

5. **Create.** We all interact with strangers every day, from the bus driver, to the woman at the post office, to someone on the train. Think back over your day and choose one of those strangers. Now create a character around your interaction with that person.

   Hint: often a great character has a telling detail that makes them memorable. It might be a scar, curly hair, a hook nose, freckles, memorable eyes, incredible strength or a photographic memory. What was it about your stranger that made you remember them?

6. **Read.** Pick up a publication you don't normally read, whether it's a newspaper, magazine, book, pamphlet, newsletter or brochure. Write a paragraph about one thing you learn from that publication.

7. **Talk.** If you're not a "queue-chatter" like Allison, today's the day to try it out. Strike up a conversation with the person waiting in line next to you. You'll quickly know if that person wants to chat back, and if they do, ask questions – people often love talking about themselves. When you get home, write a paragraph about one thing you talked about.

8. **Take note.** Writers are often encouraged to keep a journal, but a lot of people struggle with what exactly that means. A writing journal is a great place to record not just what happens in your day, but how you felt about it. You don't need to do a "woke up, went to work, had dinner" diary, but rather, choose one incident from your day and write about it in full.

   This is a brilliant way to not only create a bank of ideas, but also to have a record of authentic feelings from any given time in your life. YA authors, in particular, find diaries from their teens to be incredibly good sources of story ideas.

9. **Find a photo.** Whether it be one of your photos, a historic photo or a random photo on the internet, photographs are incredible sources of story ideas. If you know the story behind the picture, write it down in the most evocative way you can. If you don't know it, create a life for those people.

10. **Go op-shopping.** Discarded items are story ideas waiting to be discovered. If you find an unusual item in a vintage, antique or op shop, don't just think about what it is, but why it's there and who it once belonged to.

CHAPTER 7
Dealing with other people

One of the most difficult things about realising you want to be a writer – that you want to take that urge and actually write something – is telling other people. It's often those closest to us who make things the most difficult. That's not because they're mean or they hate us or they're trying to crush our dreams, but because they instinctively recognise the truth about writing.

Writing is selfish.

Announcing to family and friends that you plan to write a novel means declaring there's now something in your life that will take time away from them. Something that will make you less available.

We often talk about not having time to write, when in fact there are other forces at work. As parents, employees and responsible citizens, there will always be pressing, important things for us to do.

Writing, particularly when it's not paid, looks like a colossal waste of time to non-writers – particularly to partners who might be working long hours to keep a family afloat financially. Or to bosses who want employees on call 24/7. Or to friends who feel they haven't seen you in months.

Writing eats up hours. It's the kind of thing that can take you far away from the dirty dishes in the sink, the unmade beds and the general detritus of daily life. Far away from the paid work that needs to be done. Far away from family life at night or from friends on weekends when, after a full week at work, you simply want to immerse yourself in your current manuscript.

Writing is a selfish task because it's all about you and your work in progress. It's difficult enough to do before partners and kids enter your life, but may become even harder to put into practice once you have children. Like a cuckoo in the nest, writing is viewed as a voracious beast that has the potential to disrupt familiar routines and interfere with family time.

Children don't understand you're in full flight, on a roll, chasing down the most glorious idea you've ever had. They want their afternoon snack, right NOW, and it's time for swimming lessons, thanks.

Partners sometimes don't get why you'd want to give up quality TV time with them to get back to your computer and the juicy subplot that came to you in the shower.

Houses do not clean themselves.

And so the fledgling writer can find themselves not only trying to balance family, friends, work and all of the other things that make up daily life, they're also trying to manage guilt. The guilt that can accompany the need to embrace a story, to put in the hours and hours that are essentially the pursuit of a dream.

Partly that's because it's a dream that non-writers can often view as unattainable. Every writer has experienced the so-called friend who's only too eager to share statistics about the downturn of the book market, and the number of rejections that J.K. Rowling and Stephen King experienced before they were published.

Partly it comes from the guilt of knowing that when we write, we're in a place that's far from family life. Shutting a study door is just the physical manifestation of letting your partner and kids know you're not available to them, sometimes for the first time in their lives, and sometimes on an ongoing basis for a project that might take months and months, even years.

Partly it can be due to the fact that writing doesn't feel particularly "useful". Partners might initially be supportive, thinking you're going to pen a bestseller and buy them that tropical island they've always wanted. But as the days turn into weeks, and the first draft turns into a second and a third and so on, resentment might begin to set in.

Like any solitary pursuit – marathon runners might relate – writing takes you "away" in pursuit of your own goal. You might be physically present, in your own home even, but it doesn't take a family long to realise your attention is elsewhere.

So what do you do?

The first thing you need to realise, and we're quoting international bestselling author Fiona McIntosh here, is that nobody cares about your book. Not really.

As Fiona said in episode 246 of our podcast, "You need to actually embrace it. No-one bloody cares that you're writing a book. Not even your own family cares, because actually it's annoying when you're not there, because you're distracted. So understand that not a single publisher has asked you to write this book. Not a single person cares if you finish it. It doesn't matter that you've wanted to write all your life. No-one cares."

And while that might sound like a depressing statement, Fiona feels writers should look at the other side of the coin and embrace the idea that no-one gives two hoots about what they're doing. "Take that on and then write free of all constraints. Don't worry about what your mum thinks, don't worry about what your friends think. Don't worry about it. Because no-one cares anyway. Just sit down and write that beautiful book."

So let's assume it's true that no-one cares. How, then, do you manage the resentment that this magnificent project of yours is bound to cause?

We've got three tips for you:

1. Own the fact that your dream may impact other people.
2. Communicate why it's important to you.
3. Act like a professional.

First, you need to own your dream and the inconvenience it's going to cause. Stop hoping you'll write a book one day and be prepared to take action. If you talk about writing a book for years and years, but never actually do anything about it, those closest to you will simply roll their eyes whenever you mention it.

Once you've decided this is the time, you need to act. By act, we mean actually start writing.

And then you need to tell people what you're doing and why it's important to you.

Tell your family and friends what you're planning to do. Tell them how long you think it will take you (this has the secondary, very important effect of giving you your first deadline!). Explain how you intend to manage the project (this has another secondary and important effect of making you plan your writing time).

Let them know you understand your writing project will have ramifications in other areas of your shared lives, and that you'll listen if they tell you you've been consumed by your manuscript. In fact, for Fiona McIntosh, this is essential.

"Don't let writing define you," she says. "I find that for too many writers that come into my orbit, the writing is so important to them, it's consuming them. They're letting writing define them, when I think it's very important that you put your family first, because they're the most important thing in the world, in your life."

Be gentle with yourself when you're having these conversations and err on the side of caution. Are you really going to blast out a first draft in three months while working full-time? Are you really going to give up yoga for a year so you can write every Wednesday from 5.30 to 7pm?

Be realistic. Pressure builds when expectations aren't met. And take particular note of the section in our next chapter that deals with "stealing" time to write.

As part of these conversations, you need to communicate why this is so important to you. Friends will understand much more readily when you skip a Sunday lunch to write if they appreciate what you're trying to achieve.

Unfortunately, this also means you'll need an answer to questions such as:

Why are you wasting your time?
I've got a great story idea – why don't you write it for me?
What's the book about?
Does this mean you'll be rich?
Can you write?
Oh sure, I'd write a book but I don't have time. Aren't you busy?
And so on.

Your answers to those questions (and the many others that will come your way) depend on your motivations for writing, your personality and your tolerance levels, but be prepared for them!

This brings us to our last tip for managing other people: act like a professional. What do we mean by that? Once you put it out there that you're writing your novel, take a leaf out of the professional writer's handbook and actually write it.

Most published authors have families and jobs to manage alongside their writing careers. They've learnt to survive without the long stretches of writing time that are the supposed ideal for creating "great work". They find a way.

Allison says, "When I was writing the first draft of *The Mapmaker Chronicles*, I was also working very hard for a corporate client and writing a weekly newsletter, as well as all my usual commitments – around 8000 words a week all told. So I wasn't getting much writing done on my manuscript during the weekdays. Even my nights were starting to be non-productive because, quite simply, I was *tired*."

Allison decided to leave the house every Saturday for an hour. "I took myself to the library just after lunch," she says. "When the family protested – as they're wont to do even if you're there for every other available waking and sleeping moment – I simply explained that other mums went to yoga or the gym or wherever. They just needed to imagine that's where I was."

Author Ben Hobson had a full-time job and a young family when he wrote his debut novel, *To Become A Whale*. How did he get the book written? In episode 180 he told us that he did it by writing it at night, even if only for 30 minutes, aiming for 1000 words a day.

Emily Gale wrote her first novels while her children were young and she was working as a bookseller. "When they were little, any time I spent away from them writing, especially when I didn't have a contract, I felt the guilt of that," she told us in episode 178.

If you're struggling with this notion that your writing is somehow selfish and an inconvenience to others, that you should be spending your time doing more worthwhile things, then you need to find a way through that. If you must, do your writing at a time when it affects no-one at all, be that 5am or midnight or during your lunch hour at work.

Make it a priority. Write it on your To Do list, and don't move it around for other things. Don't put "write novel" because, frankly, that's terrifying. Put "200 words" or "500 words" or "30 minutes". Squeeze it in when you can. Squeeze hard.

Because life changes. Children grow up (even though it sometimes feels as though they'll be small forever) and as they do, that sense of guilt gets smaller.

"My children are now 13 and 10," Emily told us, "and it's just so different writing now to when they were little. I don't feel guilty anymore."

Had Emily waited until now to begin, she would not have already published three novels.

If you have stories to write, then write them. Give yourself permission, negotiate the time, manage the expectations. Let your loved ones know how important this is to you. Don't hide it from them or from anyone.

If you hide it, you won't do it.

But more than that, the fact is that you can't write a book if you don't sit down and write it. Talking about writing a book is so much more fun, but it won't get the work done. Equally, the "work" is also about more than typing.

Recognise that some of your best work in creating your story requires no pen or keyboard.

Some of the most important work of writing is the dreaming, the thinking, the tucking the story away into the back of your mind and allowing your subconscious to gnaw at it – that's work.

Remember this on those days when you feel like you're doing nothing, and you're frustrated and angry because you feel as though time is slipping away. The dreaming time is important in the writing process, and you have to classify that as writing time.

Children's author Zanni Louise told us in episode 169, "Keep your creativity close at hand. So what I mean by that is no matter how busy you are or no matter what you're doing in your life, keep being creative in no matter what function you can.

"Whether it's writing on the back of a serviette, or scribbling down things in a notebook, or writing in the mist of the mirror, just keep doing little tasks constantly. Activate those creative muscles. Then, when you do have your pockets of time when you can write, the creative juices are already flowing. I find it's much easier to then produce something."

5 steps to take today

1. Create a writing plan. This doesn't need to be elaborate or complicated, but can be as simple as getting out your diary and scheduling in some writing time. In the next chapter, we'll look at ways to steal writing time, but for now, start with the obvious and make at least one appointment with yourself for this week. Be realistic.

2. Create a writing space for yourself. This doesn't need to be perfect. It doesn't need to be large. It doesn't even need to be permanent. Just think about a quiet space you can retreat to with a notebook or a laptop when it's writing time.

3. Tell your family and friends you're writing a novel. This does two things. First, it makes you accountable (trust us, nothing will spur you on like having your nearest and dearest asking you, "How's the novel going?"). Second, it validates your endeavours. If you make it important, those around you will also make it important. This means you'll be in a better position to say no to quick weekend catch-ups which might eat into your writing time.

4. Be prepared to leave your mobile device at home. Nothing eats into dreaming time more than the constant presence of your phone or tablet. Try leaving them behind for just one day to see where your mind takes you.

5. Start writing today. Even if you think you have no time. Even if you think you don't know what you're writing. Just open a Word document or a notebook, write "My Novel" at the top, and write a sentence or two. You'll feel better. Trust us.

CHAPTER 8

Do you want to go on a date?

In today's fast-paced world, our schedules are often completely slammed. It feels like there isn't a spare moment from the minute you wake up until you lay your head back on your pillow.

Whether you're a full-time worker or a full-time parent – or have to use all your juggling skills to combine both those roles – life can end up a blur.

When this happens consistently, it's vital to ensure that our creative juices are being replenished. Why? Because as creatives we need to refuel our brains and our souls with activities and experiences that give us joy. They're like oxygen.

If we deprive ourselves of this creative oxygen, we simply wither and die.

Alright, we know that sounds a bit dramatic. But the reality is that if we don't feed our creative souls, we can eventually lose all motivation and momentum. We end up convincing ourselves that we've lost our creative mojo.

However, that's rubbish! Creativity isn't something you can lose. We all have creativity within us waiting to emerge, but if we don't nurture this part of our psyche, it won't bloom.

So what can you do to ensure your creative well is always full? Schedule regular creative dates with yourself!

What is a creative date?

A creative date is simply an appointment you make with yourself where you do something creative. This sounds very broad, but the main parameters are that the activity needs to be something you enjoy and that you can do on your own.

Ideally, it fits one of these categories:

1. **It taps into your creativity.** You might go to an art gallery, take a woodworking class, build a sandcastle.

2. **It helps you meditate or renew your energy.** Go for a walk by the creek down the road, book in for a foot massage, sample a new yoga session.

3. **It allows you to explore an activity or subject that piques your creative curiosity.** Attend a talk about war history, go to a seminar about origami, pore over books at the library about banksias.

The concept of the creative date is a variation of a concept originally inspired by the term "artist's date" coined by Julia Cameron in her book *The Artist's Way*.

One important aspect of a creative date is that you need to do it by yourself. You get the call the shots. You get to linger over a painting that you love at the art gallery without feeling the pressure to catch up with a friend who might have moved on to the next wing. You get to spread out heaps of books on the desk at the library without worrying whether your child is wreaking havoc in the kids' section.

This is your time.

How to go on a creative date

If you're wondering how in the world you can fit this in, a creative date doesn't have to take a long time. But it should be regular.

Sometimes it may take only 20 minutes. At other times it could take all day. However, a reasonable time for a creative date would be 60 to 90 minutes. Enough time so that you feel like you've done something significant, but not too long that you feel you can't fit it into your week.

If you don't live anywhere near a library, art gallery, painting workshop – or whatever activity you'd like to try – that's fine. There's always the internet! And there are countless YouTube videos, online workshops, webinars and talks that can amuse you no end. The key is to make sure it doesn't feel like a chore – you need to choose an activity that's fun.

Still don't have ideas for creative dates? This list is by no means exhaustive, but here are 30 to get you thinking. Remember, everyone is different – some will appeal to you, others won't. Just pick the ones you think would be fun and interesting.

1. Go to an art exhibition.
2. Hang out at the library and ask for their recommendations.

3. Go for a walk with your camera or phone and take photos all with the same theme.

4. Create a room or corner of your own in your home.

5. Watch that documentary you've been meaning to catch.

6. Explore a hardware store – we guarantee you won't leave empty-handed.

7. Create a vision board.

8. Do some gardening.

9. Take a watercolour workshop.

10. Make a gift – or gift card – for the next person you know who's having a birthday.

11. Attend a sound-healing workshop.

12. Learn how to massage your cat.

13. Lie on the grass and look at the clouds.

14. Search for inspiring artists on Instagram and follow them.

15. Cook up a recipe you've always wanted to try.

16. Try a sport you've always wanted to sample.

17. Have a massage or a facial.

18. Go to a writing workshop.

19. Make a playlist of your favourite songs for different activities (chilling, workout, writing, house-cleaning).

20. Go to a farmers' market.

21. Declutter one room in your house (so long as you think that's fun!).

22. Solve the crossword.

23. Go somewhere you haven't been to in ages but which has pleasant memories.

24. Go on a historical walk.

25. Make a cup of tea and sit in the garden with your journal.
26. Go to a café and people-watch.
27. Play on the equipment at a kids' playground. If you think that might be weird on your own, find an urban gym and play on that.
28. Attend an author talk and get your copy of their book signed.
29. Volunteer at a pet rescue organisation.
30. Learn how to groom your dog, cat or hamster.

Why are creative dates important?

Valerie embraced the world of creative dates a few years ago. She tried to schedule them in weekly but isn't too hard on herself if she has to skip a few here and there. Sure, during the period when her diary looks more like an extreme sport than a calendar of appointments, she may not go on a creative date for a month. But she gets them back on track as soon as she can.

And that's because she's experienced first-hand what can happen if you don't fill your creative well.

Valerie says, "I didn't even notice it happening. Slowly, bit by bit, my creative mojo started to seep away. And that can happen when you let life take over. When you're responsible for a business. When you have an obligation to a team of staff and countless customers. There are spreadsheets, cashflow projections, tax issues, scheduling, negotiations, websites to build, deals to be done and speeches to be made.

"They're all important things. And, sure, some of them are creative – if you use the word kind of loosely. But I'm talking about the exploration of creativity and expression that feeds your soul. An appreciation of art and genius and play – and the way they all combine to create a magical personal journey that can transform and inspire you – and other people."

It's important to point out that the form this soul-feeding creativity takes is different for everyone. For you, it might be music. For another, it could be painting. For someone else, it's writing. For even others, it could be business. It's the thing you're curious about. That creative itch you need to scratch. The thing that makes you smile when you're discovering more about it.

"For a couple of years, I couldn't even articulate to you what that thing was for me. My creative well was so empty that I'd forgotten how to tap into it," says Valerie.

"I know this sounds totally weird coming from someone who's the head of one of the most creative organisations in the country – where I'm surrounded by creative minds at all levels, from newbie students to the most experienced and acclaimed writers in Australia.

"But, like I said, spreadsheets, projections, websites… you get the idea. Don't get me wrong. I'm not saying that if you love spreadsheets and projections that automatically means you're in a creative desert too. Not at all. Remember, everyone is different. Your passion is totally different to mine."

Valerie had allowed herself to slip into a ridiculous and gruelling work schedule. "I reckon I probably ran a two-year marathon between 2014 and 2015 where I was so focused on work that it became my entire life. And I loved it. I really did. I wasn't unhappy. In fact, I revelled in it. It wasn't just satisfying, it was a bona fide adrenaline rush to get so much stuff done.

"While I was in it, I didn't begrudge it one bit. Pig in mud! My business was on track. I was speaking at events around the country. I was travelling, meeting people, and sharing my passion for business and writing with many others.

"Then one day I realised that in 2015, with the exception of work-related events, I'd gone out for dinner to a restaurant only four times that entire year. That's not a typo. Four times. And three of them were to the same place! Insane."

Valerie wasn't exercising, had no social life and felt like she'd lost her creative mojo. "Towards the end of 2016, I knew that I had to make a change, that I had to schedule in bouts of creativity and fun. I'd still work like a demon when I needed to, but I had to make sure I explored my creative curiosity. I started making appointments to take myself out on creative dates."

She asked an artist she admired to mentor her in her exploration of the art world. Valerie started heading to a nearby beach to journal and let the contents of her brain pour onto the pages. She moved her piano, which had been stored at her grandmother's house for 30 years, to her home. And she made a point to watch movies or documentaries about writers and artists who inspired her.

"Re-energising yourself with this creative oxygen is vital. Of course, the irony is that I give this advice all the time, but I'd forgotten to take that advice in my own creative journey.

"I had to remind myself that this advice works. It really does. Ever since I've made creative dates a priority, I've been more fulfilled. More energised. More inspired. And that creative mojo just hasn't stopped flowing."

Apart from replenishing your creative well, these dates often give you the brainspace you need for some thinking time. For writers, the work doesn't just happen at the keyboard. You solve complex plot points during a walk in the national park. You figure out how to kill that character while you're doing downward dog at yoga.

You need to meditate on your story and let it unfold in your brain. This is an essential part of the creative process, and it doesn't always happen at the computer.

Make an appointment with yourself

Do yourself a favour. Sit yourself down with a cup of tea or a glass or wine and write a list of potential creative dates you'd enjoy. Don't be tempted to ring your BFF to go with you. This is an important date you need to do on your own.

Then make this appointment in your diary and stick to it. If you really feel you can't commit to a weekly date at this point, aim for fortnightly and then reassess in a couple of months.

Go on. Trust us. Your writing – and your life – will be better for it.

CHAPTER 9
How to make time to write

When you're trying to squeeze writing into a life that's already full to the brim with work, family, friends and your myriad other commitments, it can be difficult to see where it will fit.

The number-one problem that many writers have today is simply finding the time to write.

To prove it, Allison conducted a survey, asking her community to tell her **the one** problem that she could help them with. More than half of the 300 people who responded answered, "How to get my book written."

So if you're feeling it's impossible to wedge writing into already overfull days, know that you're NOT alone.

But also know that it can be done.

As the author of *The Mapmaker Chronicles*, the bestselling series for middle-grade children, Allison wrote three 55,000 word novels within 18 months in 2014-15 – all while working regularly as a teacher, freelance writer, social media manager, and speaker, as well as managing a busy family life with all that entails.

Then, 12 months later, while working hard to promote those books as well as *still* working as a teacher, freelance writer, social media manager and speaker, she wrote another book in the *Mapmaker Chronicles* series, as well as the two *Ateban Cipher* novels.

In other words, she gets it. Allison knows what it feels like to be desperate to get to your manuscript – but to be thwarted by kids, jobs and other demands. She also knows what it feels like to *want* to write your manuscript, but to be so incredibly tired from dealing with all those demands that it just doesn't seem to happen.

The reality is that you will never find time to write your novel.

On the surface this is a very depressing statement: you will never find time to write your novel.

You have to make the time.

That means working with the time you have, not the time you wish you had.

So before we get to the "hows" of making time to write, let's look at some of the reasons why you think it can't be done.

The time is now

If you're waiting for the kids to grow up, or to leave home, or for work to get less busy, or that time when you'll be able to switch from five days to four, you will never write your book.

If you're waiting to take a week's holiday, or dreaming of winning a stay at a writing retreat, or until that moment when you can throw in your job and feel like a 'real' writer, you'll never write your book.

You have to fit it in.

This applies to writing a novel, or a short story, or that feature you'd love to see published. But let's focus for now on novel-writing, because most people find that prospect utterly overwhelming. They can't see how on earth they'll fit it into their lives.

Allison will tell you she has never put aside an entire day to write. If she did so, she'd end up cleaning the fridge and washing the windows instead. How many times have you decided you'll spend a day writing and then spent all your time procrastinating?

Over the past 20 years, Allison has written 11 published books, three unpublished romance novels, one unpublished contemporary fiction novel, two children's picture books she pulls out for editing every year, two middle-grade novels currently being edited, and one junior fiction manuscript that needs redrafting.

Until a year or two ago, all of these were her "side projects", written in and around and between countless mortgage-paying magazine articles and the full-time, then part-time, then full-time, then part-time care of two children.

These days, due to the success of the *Mapmaker Chronicles* and *Ateban Cipher* series, Allison can bring some of her fiction writing into the "paid" category of her writing business, scheduling it into regular working hours because it has deadlines. All other fiction is still pure speculation, though, and therefore she squeezes it in around other things.

The key is that if Allison had waited until she'd found time to write, she might be just starting out now – or she might not.

The truth is that there will *always* be a reason not to start. And if you don't start, you simply don't write.

Starting can be so difficult. Allison struggled with it in the beginning, because she used to believe she needed to know where something ended before she even began. This was the result of years of freelance writing, of doing interviews and research, and knowing the angle, the hook and the conclusion before she wrote a word.

These days, Allison will tell you the best ideas can happen while you're actually writing. And she knows the subconscious can draw together strings of thought and theme in surprising ways.

How does she know that? She got started.

It's only by starting that you learn how you write a novel. You'll notice we didn't say "how *to* write a novel", and the reason is that, frankly, everyone does it differently.

Remember Allison's unpublished romance novels we mentioned before. They were each between 60,000 and 90,000 words long. They represented hours and hours of writing time, thinking time and general "figuring out" time.

They will never be published, but they were Allison's start.

It's only by writing that you learn how you write. If you keep putting off the writing, then you're not doing that practice, not learning how things come together for you.

It may be that you're finding it difficult because you have no "place" to write.

Your dream of the perfect writing life may involve a little weatherboard studio, open and spacious, with big French doors opening onto a verandah wreathed in roses. Or you may daydream of a cottage by the sea, close enough to the beach to hear the waves crash and taste the salt on your tongue. Or perhaps an attic in Paris, with a view out over the rooftops.

We all have those dreams, but if you wait until this magical writing place materialises, you will never write anything.

Most published authors are making do, writing wherever and whenever they can. Allison asked a whole raft of author friends where they wrote. Their most popular responses – and these are all multi-published authors – included the kitchen table, the couch, in their bedrooms. The only one who claimed to have a "writing studio", then laughed and admitted it was a draughty shed in the backyard.

What can we take from this?

It's not the place that makes the writing special. It's the writing that makes the place special. And that means you can – and should – write anywhere.

To make time to write, you need to know exactly what's stopping you. So right now, ask yourself these two questions:

Why are you too busy?
What are you too busy doing?
Write the answers down.

We understand busy, and we understand how all-consuming busy can be. But to carve out time to write when you have a busy family and work life, you have to look at what you're being busy about.

There are certain parts of our day that are set in stone. Sorting out kids, working nine to five – our days are all different but all busy in their own ways. It's a matter of working around those essential parts, and of finding ways to be busy with things we *want* to be busy with.

To do that, you need a goal. And then you need a plan.

How to create an achievable writing goal

Let's look at the goal first. If we were to ask you about your writing goals and you said, "I want to write a novel", we'd first applaud you. Then we'd sit you down and ask, "How will you write your novel?"

It's time to be specific, because "I want to write a novel" is one of those vague statements that people put on a New Year's resolution list and forget about by January 12.

How will you do it? What will the time-frame be? When will you do it? And, perhaps most importantly of all...

What are you willing to give up to make it happen?

This is the thing, the big question. If you're going to make time to write a novel of – well, let's say it's contemporary fiction – a minimum of 70,000 words, something will need to give.

You can't write a novel by talking about it – though we do agree that talking about it can be way more fun. This means you need to commit to sitting down and writing. Yes, thinking is an important part of the process, but at some point you've got to get the thoughts out of your head and onto the page.

Create a realistic goal for yourself. Think very carefully about how much time you can realistically carve out for yourself. If it's one hour a week, chances are that your first draft will NOT be finished in six months. That's okay. This isn't a race where you have to finish first. This is about *finishing* full stop.

And this where your plan comes into place.

Allison learnt several things about herself when she was writing her first full-length novel. Her oldest son was a newborn and she was working as a freelance writer.

She learnt that she could get by on very little sleep – which is a huge bonus to someone who's trying to combine parenting, paid work and faffing about with a novel. She learnt that the middle of the night – literally, the 10pm-midnight shift – was very productive for her.

And she learnt that television really didn't interest her that much.

These are all excellent things for someone who's writing a novel around a family. They may not be your things – not everyone wants to write in the middle of the night and many of us need more sleep than that allows. But they're the sorts of things you need to think about when you're identifying those all-important times in your day that you can slip your writing into.

Heather's bite-sized pieces

Author Heather Smith has an even more systematic approach to getting the words out. Heather is author of several non-fiction books, including the runaway bestseller *Xero for Dummies*.

"I'm quite methodical in the way I write. If I'm given 55,000 words, I break that up. I perceive that as 110 x 500-word groups or blogs. I think, 'I just have to get about three points out in each of those 500 word groupings.' So I'll think about something while I'm driving in the car, or cleaning up, or something like that. I'll work out in my head what those three points are going to be.

"Then I can sit down, put them down, flesh it out, write it up. I might go and cook the dinner, then come back and edit, edit, edit. Sometimes I'll go, 'This is what I'm going to write about tomorrow.' I'll sleep on it, which is a fabulous technique for pulling together all the things you're thinking about."

Heather says she ends up with 110 little pieces, which she stitches together "like a quilt".

"When you break everything down to 500 words, that really sounds a lot more manageable," she explains.

7 strategies for making time to write

To help you, we've identified seven practical strategies for making time to write. The published authors we know use all manner of combinations of these, but to begin with, you just need to identify one that actually works for you.

For instance, there's no point in saying "I'll get up an hour earlier every day" if you know you hit the snooze button six times every morning as it is. Perhaps you could start by getting up 30 minutes earlier one day a week… or try something else!

These strategies do require discipline, though.

Discipline is a deeply unsexy word, but it's at the heart of every published novel. Somebody had the discipline to sit down and write and to keep writing until it was done. To create your own stories, you also need to create routines.

Routines may not be cool. They may not photograph well on Instagram or play well in dinner party stories, but they help you to get the work done when you're a writer.

1. Get up early

We know several authors, including international bestselling author Kate Forsyth, who wake up at 5am and do a couple of hours of writing before the day even begins. Doing it this way means you get it done before heading out to work, when you're fresh and before anyone even notices you're missing from the family landscape – and with fewer interruptions.

2. Stay up late

Like getting up early, this won't work for everyone, but it works for Allison and countless other authors. It may be that the last thing you feel like doing after a day of work is sitting down at a desk to write, but, as Allison will tell you, the key is just to get there and get started.

3. Write 500 words a day

Allison interviewed the author Annabel Smith – a mother of one, with a day job as teacher of English as a second language – for the podcast. She was surprised to discover that Annabel, the author of three novels at the time and counting, writes 500 words every day. No more and no less.

Even if she's in the middle of the most exciting idea in the universe, she stops at 500. As Annabel puts it, it means that she always knows where to start the next time she sits down. It's a technique that the English novelist Graham Greene used – he wrote 500 words a day, every day of his life – and we can definitely see how it could work for many writers.

That's because 500 words is not an overwhelming amount. It's the equivalent of eating an elephant one bite at a time. If you wrote 500 words a day for an entire year, you'd have 182,500 by the end. If you only wrote on weekdays, you'd still have 130,000. That's more than enough to be the first draft of a novel.

If 500 is too difficult, try 200 words. If you do it every day, you'll get 73,000 words, basically a commercial-length manuscript. If you do it five days a week, you'll have 52,000 – it might take you 18 months to finish the manuscript but, still, 18 months from now, you'll have finished a novel.

4. Steal time where you can

Children's author Tristan Bancks, father of two, told our podcast he writes every morning – as he walks along the beach. He literally types 2000 words on his phone while he's walking, combining his daily exercise with his writing time.

Tristan, and countless other authors, write their novels in whatever time they can steal. This is not to say that stolen moments are necessarily spontaneous moments.

Sue Whiting, for example, wrote an entire novel during her commute on the train.

In fact, one of the best ways to squirrel time for writing is to make those stolen moments part of your routine. If the only time you can steal during the day is on your commute to work, then make an appointment with yourself to write your 200, 500 or however many words you can during that time.

If you find yourself waiting outside swimming lessons once a week for half an hour, take your laptop or notepad with you and sit in the car and write.

5. Get the draft down

When you have limited time, you need to focus on moving the story forward. There are two types of writers – pioneers or discoverers, who rush ahead to new territory all the time – and settlers – who will get to a new scene and explore a bit. Allison is a pioneer. When she has the bit between her teeth with a story, she goes forward, mostly because she can't wait to see what happens next.

You might be a settler, wanting to dig in a bit, poke around, make things look beautiful before you move on.

Both of these approaches are fine. But if you want to finish your manuscript, constant editing and re-editing as you write will not get you there. We've both spoken to writers who've been working on polishing their first three chapters for months, because they've heard that these need to be the best and that they're what an agent or publisher will judge the story on. Our response is always, "Okay, and then what are you going to do if they ask to see a full manuscript? Do you even know what happens next?"

Editing is essential. There's no doubt about that. But endless editing is not helping you to get the story finished, particularly when you have only scraps of time in which to write it. Get the whole story down, to the point where you're happy to type "The End", and then go back to the beginning and refine, redraft and rewrite.

6. Leave home

While this might be tempting, particularly after reading the previous chapter, we're not suggesting you leave behind your distractions forevermore. Rather, that you make a regular appointment to leave the house to write.

You might decide to go to a café or a hot-desk space or wherever works for you. If you're finding it difficult to get the writing done at home, make an appointment with yourself to go somewhere else. And then keep it, exactly as you would if you were heading out to the gym, to yoga or any of the other places that people go regularly.

7. Make yourself accountable

If you're struggling to fit the writing in, you need to make yourself accountable, and for that you need some writing friends. If you're already busy, you may think the last thing you need is to add in meetings with a writers' group. We'd agree with that.

But you do need some form of accountability.

In the early days of her fiction writing career, Allison joined an online writing group as part of the Romance Writers of Australia organisation. (Incidentally, she can't recommend RWA highly enough for anyone writing romance, commercial or contemporary women's fiction – or anything along those lines.)

She was matched with two women she'd never met. Suddenly she had two people expecting to read 2000 words from her every month – and the motivation to achieve at least that number. With expectations on her (and a deadline), Allison found she could make progress. Previously it had been all too easy to put the writing off because she thought she had no time to do it.

These days, you can create your own group thanks to Twitter or Facebook, or join an established group or organisation. You could, for example, have a look at National Novel Writing Month, or NaNoWriMo as it's known. This international challenge takes place every November and the aim is to write 50,000 words in 30 days, complete with group interaction, graphs, "write-ins" at local libraries and more.

You may not reach 50,000 words in 30 days, but any words you have at the end of November are a win if you're struggling to make progress with your manuscript. You'll find more details about NaNoWriMo at nanowrimo.org.

7 essential books on writing and creativity

If a writers' group or online challenge is not your idea of fun, you can still learn from other writers. How? From books.

We often talk on the podcast about the importance of reading widely, and that includes reading about writing. So we've created a list of our favourite seven must-read books about writing and creativity.

Some of these encompass the writers' journey, others are simple "how to" books, because the fact is that learning to write well helps you to make the most of any time that you have to write.

You're sure to find other books about writing that work for you, but here's our list to get you started:

1. *On Writing: A Memoir of the Craft*, by Stephen King
2. *Bird by Bird: Some Instructions on Writing and Life*, by Anne Lamott
3. *The Writing Book*, by Kate Grenville
4. *The Artist's Way: A Spiritual Path To Higher Creativity*, by Julia Cameron
5. *Big Magic: Creative Living Beyond Fear*, by Elizabeth Gilbert
6. *Writing Down The Bones: Freeing the Writer Within*, by Natalie Goldberg
7. *The War of Art: Winning the Inner Creative Battle*, by Steven Pressfield

Tools to help you make time to write

In many ways, it's never been easier to be a writer. It's ridiculous how many gadgets and devices there are these days – it can be overwhelming.

Many writers still use a notebook. Kate Forsyth, for instance, keeps one big notebook for each book she writes. When she has an idea for a novel, she gets out a fresh, new notebook, writes down everything she can think of about that story, and then puts it away to *finish the project she's working on.*

This is important. If you're constantly distracted by bright, shiny, new ideas, you'll never complete a novel. Finish what you start. Get the draft down. Then go and write something else while the draft sits there and matures. By the time you go back to edit it, you'll be able to see it clearly.

But there are many other ways, and not everyone wants to write longhand. While a notebook is a very portable writing tool, technology means your manuscript can be just a click away at all times on a range of different devices.

We've provided you with a list of tech tools in a later chapter. The key is to experiment until you find solutions that are right for you.

Our top 10 tips for getting the words written

"A year from now you will wish you had started today." You've probably heard these words 1000 times, but now it's time to sit up and take notice.

1. Make writing a priority

If you're always saying, "I'm going to write a novel one day," realise that day is today. Stop waiting for conditions to be perfect and start putting down "writing" in your diary.

2. Make yourself accountable

Tell people you're writing. Nothing will galvanise you into action faster than a whole bunch of friends asking you how the novel is going.

3. Decide what you're willing to give up

Do you really need to watch the latest reality TV trainwreck, or can you simply keep up with it through the recaps posted just hours after each episode? Can you skip one gym session a week? Are you able to send the rest of the family to that catch-up with friends while you stay home to write?

4. Set a realistic writing goal

This is what 500 words a day looks like:

500 words 500 words

500 words 500 words

500 words words

500 words 500 words 500 words 500 words 500 words 500 words 500 words 500 words 500 words 500 words 500 words 500

words 500 words 500 words 500 words 500 words 500 words 500
words 500 words 500 words 500 words 500 words 500 words 500
words 500 words 500 words 500 words 500 words 500 words 500
words 500 words 500 words 500 words

500 words 500 words 500 words 500 words 500 words 500
words 500 words 500 words 500 words 500 words 500 words 500
words 500 words 500 words 500 words 500 words 500 words 500
words 500 words 500 words 500 words 500 words 500 words 500
words 500 words 500 words 500 words 500 words 500 words 500
words 500 words 500 words 500 words 500 words 500 words

500 words 500 words 500 words 500 words 500 words 500
words 500 words 500 words 500 words 500 words 500 words 500
words 500 words 500 words 500 words 500 words 500 words 500
words 500 words 500 words 500 words 500 words 500 words 500
words 500 words 500 words 500 words 500 words

500 words 500 words 500 words 500 words 500 words 500
words 500 words 500 words 500 words 500 words 500 words 500
words 500 words 500 words 500 words 500 words 500 words 500
words 500 words 500 words 500 words 500 words 500 words 500
words 500 words 500 words 500 words 500 words 500 words

500 words 500 words 500 words 500 words 500 words 500
words 500 words 500 words 500 words 500 words 500 words 500
words 500 words 500 words 500 words 500 words 500 words 500
words 500 words 500 words 500 words 500 words 500 words 500
words 500 words 500 words

Have a look. Work out how many of those you could write each and every time you sit down. This is a realistic writing goal. It may be that your goal is 200 words (four paragraphs like this one) and that's okay. As long as you do it regularly.

5. Identify and use the dead time in your day

- If you commute on a train or bus, look at the tools available to help you write on the run and use them.
- If you drive to work, can you use dictation software to get your ideas down?
- If you're in a doctor's waiting room, don't read 10-year-old magazines, write your own stories.
- If your kids have regular sports training sessions, miss watching one a week and stay in the car to write.

6. Create a routine

Stealing time from the cracks and slips in your day is one way to make time. But the most effective way is to build writing into your daily routine. Work out which end of the day will work for you and either get up early or stay up late. If you have a young family, write during afternoon nap time or swap an hour's babysitting with a friend who might also like some creative time.

7. Use the tools available to help you

An old-fashioned notebook is still an incredibly portable writing tool, but if, like Allison, you can't read your own handwriting, look at some of the other tools available. That way, when you do get that 30 minutes at soccer training, you'll be able to take full advantage of it.

8. Seek out support

Like-minded people will help you to achieve your goals. Find other writers to help cheer you on – people who understand what you're trying to achieve, will help make you accountable and will offer strategies that work for them. Just remember that talking about writing is not writing, so make sure you're writing as well as all the rest!

9. Commit to writing forward

If you're continually editing the words you've written, you'll struggle to finish your manuscript – and if you don't finish, it will never be published. If you're working on your first draft, write forward, don't keep going back, over and over what you've written.

10. Start today

Remember, if you need next-level help with this, Allison has created the Creative Writing 30-Day Bootcamp. It will help you to establish a writing habit *and* deliver 10,000-plus words if you follow her advice and instructions each day. Find out more at writerscentre.com.au/bootcamp.

10,000 words. Don't just imagine it – do it!

CHAPTER 10
How to be creative when you're tired

How many times have you told yourself you're too tired to even consider writing? That you'll start tomorrow? That you don't have a coherent thought in your head, let alone a creative one?

We've all been there.

Life can be exhausting, physically and emotionally. We feel it too. But if writing a book – or a short story, or a feature – is something you really want, there's no getting around the fact that it needs to be written. Even when you're tired.

We've already given you strategies on how to make time to write, and tips and tricks for getting the words on the page. But overcoming fatigue is a whole different part of the equation, and it can be a real struggle when our lives get busy.

So what can we do?

The first thing is to get over the idea that you have to be *feeling* creative to *be* creative. In a perfect world, we'd all wake up bright and early every morning, full of vim and vigour, with the Muse perched on our shoulders and a mind full of creative thoughts.

This almost never happens.

You cannot wait for the Muse. As Allison often says, "She's held up in traffic. Start without her".

What we mean is that you cannot wait for creativity to strike, for a genius idea to drop down from the clouds. You have to start writing – even when you don't feel like it.

Every published author we've interviewed on our podcast will tell you that "the work" is the key.

"There's no substitute for the work," Charlotte Wood told us.

"I find writing to be hard work, and I often wish I didn't feel obliged or compelled to write," Kyle Ladd lamented.

Writing is work. Yes, it's a wonderful thing when it's all coming together and you're immersed in the joy of the story. But putting together 50,000 or 70,000 or 100,000 words is not all fun and giggles (sadly).

Which is why, if you listen to the hundreds of author interviews on our podcast, you'll hear one word repeated over and over again: routine.

Routines are not cool. They're not sexy. They do not photograph well and they most certainly do not fit the ideal of the wafty creative writer wandering about in a cloud of inspiration or dreaming in cafés.

What routines do, however, is get the work done. Whether you're feeling creative or not. Whether you're tired or not. If you can create yourself a routine – a habit, if you like – then you'll write the words.

Read over our tips for making time to write, and then create a routine for yourself. And while you've got your diary out, think about a few of these things as well, which will help you to be creative when you're tired.

A writer is not all you are

While it's tempting to fill every bit of free or stolen time with writing, it's not sustainable. Be realistic about what you can manage. If you're feeling really tired, pull back. Write three times a week instead of five. Or once a week instead of three times.

Remember the importance of making time to fill that creative well. It's one thing to say no to coffee dates to steal writing time, but balance this with the importance of keeping your support networks in place. Coffee dates can help revive your spirits.

As Fiona McIntosh told us in episode 264, "You should have hobbies or interests that take you away from your writing, because it's too easy to get so wrapped up in your storytelling that you become one dimensional and boring.

"Understand that one of the beautiful aspects of you is that you can write a story. Or that you hear stories in your mind. Celebrate that, and go forward with that. Don't let it become so all-consuming that it twists you in knots and sucks away at your confidence."

Exercise

We know what you're thinking: "I'm too tired to write, why would I suddenly take up jogging?"

The truth is, however, that there's a link between movement and creativity.

Allison, a keen walker with her dog Procrastipup, was thrilled by the findings of a Stanford University study. Researchers Marily Oppezzo and Daniel L. Schwartz carried out four experiments and demonstrated that "walking boosts creative ideation in real time and shortly after".

The 2014 study was published in the American Psychological Society's *Journal of Experimental Psychology: Learning, Memory and Cognition*. We discussed it on the podcast in 2015 because Allison was so excited to see formal research underpin what she'd always believed – that repetitive movement (or "active meditation" as she likes to call it) unlocks the creative process.

Allison says, "I write and talk a lot about the benefits of exercise for my writing. When I do writing workshops in schools, I always tell the kids that if they're struggling to think of an idea for a story, they need to go for a walk around the block or, if they really want to excite their mums, weed the garden."

She explains that it's all about "having your body focus on a task that's kind of dull, leaving your brain free to wander".

Exercise is good for us – not just for our bodies, but our minds. You don't need to go far to find an article, study or entire thesis that supports this statement. We could cite a whole barrage of scientific research about endorphins, energy levels, [insert the positive benefits of the exercise of your choice], but this is not about suddenly taking up a whole new workout routine in the pursuit of creativity.

Movement is what you need. If you're feeling tired and as though you don't have a creative bone in your body, try a walk or some other kind of rhythmic exercise. Domestic chores kill two birds with one stone.

Still don't believe us? Maybe this will convince you:

"The best time for planning a book is while you're doing the dishes."
— Agatha Christie

Remove the publishing imperative

"I'm going to be published by the time I'm [insert age of choice] or I'll [insert dire consequence of choice]."

This notion that there's a certain age by which publishing success is defined is nothing new. How often do we see a story about a young prodigy who's been published at 17, or 15, or... six? (Seriously, Christopher Beale was six years old in 2006 when he landed the title of world's youngest novelist after his 1500-word, five-chapter novel was published in the UK.)

On top of that, by the age of 35 or 40, authors are excluded from applying for young writers' prizes.

Even if you're not actively aware of it, this all adds a level of pressure to be published, which is exhausting in itself.

The key thing to remember is that the age by which you publish your first book is not important.

Toni Morrison wrote her first novel at 39.

Richard Adams was 54 when *Watership Down* was published.

J.R.R. Tolkien's first novel, *The Hobbit*, was published when he was 45.

E. Annie Proulx was 57 when her first novel, *Postcards*, was published.

Hilary Spiers told us she was 61 when she first started writing her hit novel *Hester and Harriet*.

What's important is giving yourself enough time and space to create a work of publishable standard – and then more time and space to make it great. It might take you six weeks to write that first draft. It might take you six years. But when you finally hold your book in your hand, your first thought will not be, "Oh, but I'm 31 [or 42, or 53, or whatever]. I missed my deadline."

It will simply be, "Oh, my!"

When you remove the publishing imperative from your writing, you allow yourself room to make mistakes. Not every word needs to be perfect right now, so even if you're tired today, you can afford to add 200 words or 500 words to your manuscript – or even just to make some notes.

If work and family and that hideous To Do list are overwhelming you, cut yourself a bit of slack. Create a new writing routine that puts you at your desk once a week for the next couple of months, until you can find your way through this particular rough patch.

What we usually find when we do this is that it allows our subconscious room to breathe. To make connections. To fire away, creating new pathways through the story.

The manuscript begins to call us back again. We make notes so that when we do have time to write, we know exactly what to do.

Embrace your tired self

Creativity is a strange and wondrous beast, liable to drop in on us when we least expect it. Or at least that's what a 2011 study by Mareike Weith and Rose Zacks published in the journal *Thinking & Reasoning* confirmed.

The study was titled "Time of day effects on problem solving: When the non-optimal is optimal". It found that tasks involving creativity might "benefit from a non-optimal time of day" with regards to our circadian rhythms.

What does this mean? It suggests that innovation and creativity are at their peak when we're not at our best.

Basically, we're at our most creative when we're tired. If you identify as a "morning person", those early hours are great for analytical and logical problem-solving. However, your most creative and innovative solutions might be found in the evening – and vice versa for the night owls among us.

When she's creating artworks, Valerie works a lot at night. During the day, she's a logical, analytical powerhouse in her role as CEO of the Australian Writers' Centre. By night, she channels her energy into her writing and her artwork. She often works in the wee morning hours, when the creative side of her brain well and truly takes over.

Allison is a night owl (though not as late, she admits, as she used to be). When her children were young, the daytime hours were for family business and her freelance writing – the paid work. Nights were for writing the things she wanted to write.

These days, she uses the mornings for creative thinking, plotting and planning in her head while walking the dog, before returning to her desk to write and manage the day-to-day tasks of her business (every published author is a small business). Afternoons are for family business, late evenings are for social media and organising the next day.

The main takeaway from this? Write even though you're tired. Even though you think you'll end up writing absolute drivel, what you end up with might be more creative than you imagine.

And remember, even 200 words plus 200 words plus 200 words all add up.

5 ways to spark your creativity

1. Allow yourself to be bored

We talked about this a little bit in the chapter on making time to write, but it's worth repeating here, where it really counts. When you're constantly stimulated by other people's output – words, pictures, thoughts, opinions – you're not leaving enough room in your brain to conjure up your own.

Leave space in your day for the dreaming, the thinking, the drifting. When we're left to do our own thing for even two minutes these days, our first impulse is to pick up a device. Don't do it.

Sit with that uncomfortable feeling of having nothing to do. Observe what's going on around you. Allow your mind to drift to a story you're working on or an idea you've had.

Creativity feeds on boredom.

2. Give yourself a reason to write

When Allison goes into schools to talk to kids about writing, she tells them there are two reasons why she loves writing. The first is that when you write, you control the whole world. Nothing happens in your story that you don't want to happen. Yes, people talk about characters taking over, but where do those characters come from? That's right, they come from you.

Even as adults, this notion of "control of the universe" is attractive. If you can control nothing else in your day – and, let's face it, who controls every single thing that happens to them? – you can control what happens on that page.

Remember this when you've had a bad day and you're tired and over it. Go to your work in progress and take back control.

3. Give yourself the tools to write

You don't know what you don't know. Valerie uses this expression a lot – it's the reason she founded the Australian Writers' Centre in the first place. We've both been immersed in words our entire lives, but we still take courses, read books about writing, listen to podcasts and learn from others.

If you're feeling tired and finding it hard to front up to your writing, blast away the cobwebs by taking a short course or even a seminar. You'll not only learn new things, you'll also draw energy and inspiration from your teacher and the other students – even in an online environment.

Writing can be a lonely task. The only person driving your project forward is you. Take a moment to learn a new way forward – and find some support along the way.

4. Take yourself on a creative date. No, really. See the earlier chapter on this!

5. Read a book outside of your usual taste. If you usually read non-fiction, pick up a book of poetry. If your taste runs to serious literary fiction, try a romance novel. If you like memoir, try a children's novel. One of the most often-cited pieces of writing advice is just one word – read – and it's true that if you're writing children's fiction, you need to read a lot of current children's fiction to get an idea of what's out there.

But if you really want to spark your creativity, read other things. Things you wouldn't necessarily read. Because they show you a different way to think and to develop ideas.

When she's writing her children's adventure novels, Allison

reads a lot of adult crime fiction. Why? Because the success of a crime novel rests on a strong connection between tight plot and character development. She doesn't take notes as she reads, but Allison knows she's absorbing and taking on board the story's rhythm and beats. The structure.

Does it end up in her own work? Not directly, but Allison will also tell you that, as a writer, she's the sum total of the thousands and thousands of different books she's read.

And you simply never know where the spark of an idea will come from.

CHAPTER 11
Technology is your friend

The world of writing can sometimes seem really analogue. There are romantic images of a writer pecking on the keys of a retro typewriter as words pour out of her soul onto the paper. And the familiar clacking of the keys and the sharp ding as she sweeps the carriage from left to right once her sentence reaches the margin.

If you're too young to relate to the above, you might see it in the movies! But as romantic as this notion is, the reality is that we live in the 21st century and there are countless technological tools at our disposal to help us write effectively and productively.

Valerie still writes longhand in certain circumstances – when she's in a café, for instance, and feels like masquerading as J.K. Rowling penning a blockbuster book series. Allison rarely does, though, mostly due to the fact that she can't read her own handwriting!

Overall though, we're both big proponents of technology. What specifically do we use?

A computer and Microsoft Word

One brilliant truth about being a writer is that the barriers to entry are ridiculously low. You basically need a computer, Microsoft Word and a connection to the internet. Almost everyone already has these items! Even if you don't, you can easily go to a library to access them – or borrow them from a friend.

You don't have to invest in lots of equipment to make a go of it. You're not a personal trainer who needs access to a decent cache of gym equipment to succeed. Or a photographer who has to invest in expensive cameras, lenses and lights just to get started. Or a florist who needs to fork out money for flowers (which don't even keep!) to offer their services.

Recently, Valerie decided to explore the world of art. "I spent more money on materials and equipment in my first month as a visual artist than I did in two decades as a writer," she says. "I was in shock!"

Life as a writer is wonderfully inexpensive.

Dropbox, Google Drive and keyboards
dropbox.com and google.com/drive

When you start taking yourself seriously as a writer, you realise you often have to write in what Allison refers to as "snatched time". This is particularly true if you're juggling a day job with raising a family, taking kids to soccer and trying to pen an article or manuscript. You don't always have the luxury of a block of hours in the day that you can dedicate solely to writing.

You might be grabbing 20 minutes before breakfast at the kitchen table with your iPad or laptop. Then another 15 minutes sitting in the car while you're waiting for your kids after school. Or 30 minutes in a café during your work lunchbreak.

If that's the case, you need technology to work for you. And that means making sure you can access your documents in the cloud from any device.

We're big fans of the cloud. You can use any number of tools, but we recommend Dropbox or Google Drive.

With tools like these, you can instantly access the piece of writing you're working on, no matter where you are. That means you don't have to wait until you're back at a particular computer because that's the only place you can find your document. It also means you can type straight into it when inspiration strikes.

Valerie says setting up all her files in the cloud using Google Drive has been instrumental in upping her productivity. "I've written in doctor's waiting rooms, on the train, in cafés, in my backyard, even during the interval at the opera," she says.

Allison adds that she couldn't live without her iPad keyboard so she can write while on the go. And Valerie even bought a foldable keyboard for her iPhone so she could fit them both into her pocket on her morning walks to the beach.

Trello

trello.com

Trello is an online index card system that can be useful for freelance writers to keep track on the progress of their stories. Let's say you come up with a story idea. Create an index card for the idea and drag it into an "ideas" column. Every time you think of a new idea, create a new index card and jot down any notes that will help you when you're ready to flesh that idea out more fully.

Once you're ready to pitch a story idea to an editor, you can move the index card to a column called "pitches in progress" so you can keep track of which pitches you're still waiting to hear back about from editors. You can note down which editor you've sent it to and when you think is a good date to follow up if you haven't had a response.

Once an editor commissions you, you can move it to a "work in progress" file and then go about researching material and interviewing case studies. You can even store links to the research on your index card.

Then, once you've submitted the story to the editor, you can move the index card to a "filed" column. And so on.

You can create any kind of workflow like this and tailor the columns to suit your specific creative process.

The beauty of Trello is that you have an at-a-glance view of the status of all your articles. If things are looking a bit thin in your "ideas" column, you'll need to get cracking on generating more. Or if you don't have many "pitches in progress", it's time to contact editors.

While a tool like Trello doesn't help you craft your sentences better, it gives you a birds-eye view of the status of your articles so you can manage your workflow more effectively.

Scrivener

writewithscrivener.com

If you're writing long-form pieces like novels or non-fiction books, then Scrivener is an effective tool that's been designed just for authors. It's not as suitable if you're writing shorter pieces, like articles. For that, use Microsoft Word.

However, Scrivener is a great tool that makes it easy to move scenes around, manage multiple timelines, keep research files in a structured form, develop characters, use index cards, format your manuscript as an eBook – and much more. The features are too many to list!

Bestselling author Natasha Lester uses Scrivener for all her manuscripts and has even developed a course for the Australian Writers' Centre to show authors how it's used in real life. In the course, 2 Hours to Scrivener Power, she shares screenshots from her novel so you can see how she uses the tool with an actual manuscript.

Natasha says, "The books I write have dual timelines, plus each timeline has a main plot and a secondary love story subplot that I like to keep track of. I use Scrivener's label feature to do this so I can easily see at a glance how often I'm alternating between timelines, and also between main plot and subplot within each timeline.

"This means I can quickly tell if one timeline has gone on for too long, or if I've forgotten the subplot entirely, or any of the other pacing problems that might occur when juggling multiple story strands."

"With its threaded corkboard, so long as I've applied a label to each scene, I can isolate just one timeline or just the main plot or just the subplot and see its progression on the corkboard," Natasha explains.

"The corkboard will show me each scene divided into separate threads: one thread for each timeline and one thread for each plot and subplot. This makes it so much easier to keep track of the pace within each story strand, as well as the pace overall."

Google Alerts

google.com/alerts

This is a great tool for freelance or content writers who want to keep up-to-date with certain topics or issues. For example, you might be writing stories about childhood obesity. It can be time-consuming and overwhelming to keep up with all the literature out there and stay on top of current discussions and research.

In order to catch the articles that are relevant, set a Google Alert for "childhood obesity" and Google will notify you whenever it indexes a new article that contains that phrase.

It's free to use Google Alerts, and once you've moved on from the topic you were interested in, you can simply delete that alert and the notifications will stop.

Google Street View

google.com/streetview

If you're writing a novel that's set in a country you're not that familiar with, Google Street View is your friend. Margaret Morgan is the author of the highly acclaimed novel *The Second Cure*, which is also being made into a television series. She keeps her files in Scrivener, including pictures of the place she's writing about.

"I keep my files in Scrivener and make sure I've always got a record of my ideas," Margaret says. "And for places where I'm setting stories, I'll take photos or find photographs of places on Google Street View and put them in the document too, so I can immerse myself in the world I'm creating."

Trove

trove.nla.gov.au

Beware of the rabbit hole that is Trove! You'll love this incredible resource, but Valerie admits she has to stop herself from delving into it too often. She's lost too many hours exploring its countless historical documents.

It's an online service run by the National Library of Australia, so you don't have to turn up at the front desk in Canberra with your library card. You can use it from the comfort of your home – or anywhere you have internet access.

Trove is home to 210 million Australian newspaper articles, almost 600,000 maps, 2.8 million government gazettes and 450,000 diaries and letters. You can access Australia's first published newspaper, the *Sydney Gazette*, from 1803.

If you're writing any kind of history piece, Trove will be one of your greatest assets. And if you're writing historical fiction, it will become a vital component in making your stories come alive with authenticity.

Just be careful – it's addictive!

Google Voice Typing

If you're struggling to find time to write but you spend a lot of time in the car, you might find this useful. It's voice-recognition that translates voice to text, so you can speak your novel out loud as you drive or even walk (assuming you don't mind talking to yourself in public).

Valerie uses Google Voice Typing when she isn't able to type. It comes free with Google Docs and transcribes your words as you talk.

"It might not be 100 per cent accurate, but it's good enough if I want to get a bunch of ideas down in a hurry," she says.

Even if you don't want to write a full novel this way, it's important to get used to recording your thoughts and impressions. Remember the chapter where we talked about finding ideas? Don't lose a moment of inspiration by failing to write them down – you *might* remember them, but then again...

Of course, you can use a notebook or the notes function on your phone to write down snippets. But these dictation tools are a quick way to record your thoughts just by speaking them.

Store impressions, character details, conversations you overhear on the train – all the fodder a writer ever needs. And so much more accessible than a Word doc on your computer at home.

Freedom, SelfControl and RescueTime
freedom.to, selfcontrolapp.com and rescuetime.com

Procrastination is the enemy of every time-poor writer – and it's a difficult enemy to conquer.

As writers, we're often our own biggest enemies. If you truly cut down to the heart of your time problems, you may find you're not making the most of the time you do have.

We joke on our podcast about procrasticleaning, procrastibaking and procrastieverything else. Heck, why do you think Allison nicknamed her dog Procrastipup?

The truth of the matter is that the only person who can beat procrastination is you. But that's not to say there isn't help available.

The internet is widely regarded as one of the biggest time-stealers of all time. It's insidious, it's everywhere and it's so very difficult to get away from when one of the tools of your trade is a computer.

Using an app that will lock you out of the internet for set periods of time is a great way to turn your focus back to your writing in those precious moments you have.

Apps such as Freedom and SelfControl will keep you away from specific sites on the internet (think Facebook, Twitter and other social media platforms) or will block access to the internet altogether, depending on your requirements.

You may be thinking, "I don't need to lock myself out of social media – I only spend five minutes on Facebook a day." This may be true, but to get a clear picture of just how you're using your time, try the RescueTime app.

It's a time-management tool that runs in the background on your computer and mobile devices and tracks the time you spend on applications and websites. It gives you an accurate picture (including reports) of how your day is spent. It will show when you're productive – and when you're distracted.

Toggl

toggl.com

If you're a copywriter or any other kind of writer who charges by the hour, you need an accurate way to ensure you record your time.

When you use Toggl, you can select when you're starting work with a particular client and the timer will run on your computer. When you're done, you stop the timer and can classify who that time should be charged to and any other details you want to record. It's very useful if you need to itemise how you've spent your time on an invoice to a client.

Even if you don't charge your clients by time, you can use this tool to determine how much time you're spending on each article you're writing so you can analyse whether you're being efficient enough. Toggl can show how much time you spent on each activity of researching, interviewing, writing and editing.

It might surprise you to discover that it took 20 hours to write an article that you'd estimated would only take you four hours. When you track and analyse your time, you'll be able to make better decisions on what to prioritise and which jobs will yield the highest return.

Penzu

penzu.com

We all know the saying that we need to have "a room of one's own". Well, in this digital age, we also reckon you need a small space on the internet that you can call your own.

Penzu is an online journal that's designed to be private. We think this is important because one of the liberating aspects of writing is that we can literally pour our thoughts and ideas onto the page without worrying if someone else is going to read it – and without having to censor ourselves.

It's a process that can be cathartic but also creatively freeing. However, you might feel you can't let yourself do this without *any* inhibitions in a Word document or a longhand journal that may end accidentally end up in the hands of someone who shouldn't be reading it.

In that case, you'd miss out on the wonderful experience of being able to truly unload your thoughts and transfer the story that's in your head and onto the page in a truly unfettered way.

That's why we like Penzu. You'll need a password to get into the app. Then *another* password to get into any of the journals you create within the app. It's like keeping your diary under lock and key – only much more secure!

CHAPTER 12
What do you really want?

When you're in a nine-to-five job that's not fulfilling your creative passions, it's easy to dream of throwing it all in and becoming a full-time writer. Particularly when you're trying to sandwich your writing in around a whole host of other things.

However, the reality is that the average amount an Australian author earns from their writing is $12,900 a year. This figure comes from a three-year study conducted by Professor David Throsby, funded by the Australian Research Council and Macquarie University, and published in 2015.

The study, called "The Australian book industry: Authors, publishers and readers in a time of change", surveyed around 1000 authors and also found that the average total income for authors, including all sources of income, is $62,000.

"All sources of income" included teaching, other creative practices not related to writing and occupations unrelated to writing.

It's a sobering picture if you're dreaming of doing nothing whatsoever beyond writing fiction for the rest of your days. But read on, there's hope! In fact, we know many writers who are earning extremely healthy incomes in excess of six figures.

Why does a writer's life have to look like that?

There's a notion that unless you're writing books and nothing but books every minute of the day, you're somehow not a "successful author". That if you have to demean yourself with other work, you've somehow failed. Or that if you've begun a career as a freelance writer and you're not immediately working nine to five every day on that, then you're somehow not a success.

We say… well, to put it politely, that's simply not true.

We've already looked at the different types of writer you can be, and the fact that you can build a portfolio of styles, but it's time to get into the nitty gritty of how you're going to make writing a part of your life.

Can you make a living from being a writer?

The short answer to this question is YES. However, the longer answer will always be another question: what does "a living" look like to you?

For most of us, the dream of making a living as a writer is "just writing". Sitting there, every day, making up stories. The reality, of course, often includes mortgages, regular bills and other financial commitments. Reality is a place where the cost of living is high and the amount of money you'd need to live that writing dream is out of reach (see the "average earnings directly from writing" quoted above).

But do you even know the true cost of your current reality, let alone your dream life?

The truth is that most people believe they'll need more money to live the life they want than they actually do – whether they're writers or not. Why? Because they start at the wrong point. They look at what they're earning now – say $100,000 – and think they'll need at least that (probably more) to live the life they want.

What you actually need to do, however, is look at how much you spend – and then examine how much you'll really need to live your dream life.

So break down your essential expenses. How much is your rent or mortgage each month? How much are you currently spending on regular bills? Can you spend less?

We're talking, of course, about that most boring of words, budgeting. But the truth is that if you truly want to change your life, to chase your dreams, to be a writer, then you need to look at the hard facts of your current life first.

Cost it out. If you do that, you might find you have the room to talk to your boss about working four days a week, instead of five, freeing up one day to write. You might discover you can afford to have your kids minded for a few hours every Thursday afternoon, creating enough time to write 2000 words a week.

If you cost it out, you can see what's possible. You can also see what you might need to change to create the world that you want. Perhaps you'll find the money to do that writing course you've been thinking about, or go to that conference, allowing you to meet other writers and take one more step along the path to your dream.

The fact is that writers do make a living – but it might be a living made up of several different income streams. Allison, for instance, makes money from book advances, royalties and sales, but she also creates courses, teaches writing and is a popular paid speaker.

She's added each of these income streams one step at a time. She transitioned from full-time work as a magazine journalist, to part-time work with a freelance component, to full-time freelance, to full-time freelance with books added, to part-time freelance with books, teaching and speaking added, to full-time working as an author, course creator, teacher and speaker.

All of this happened over the course of ten years.

Ten years.

Not overnight.

Plan for a long career

There are, of course, authors who sell one book and their lives change forever. These are the ones we read about in the papers. They're the ones who inspire the dream. But overnight success stories make the papers precisely because they're newsworthy. And they're newsworthy because they're rare.

So dream of being one of those headline stories – but plan for a long career.

Planning means looking at your dream step by step, creating goals along the way. If you need a reminder about this, see the rules at the beginning of this book, particularly the one that says, "It starts as a side hustle."

Begin by working with the time you have, not the time you wish you had – which means starting to write your book NOW and taking steps to build your profile as an author as well. This is where you do your budget and look at whether you can actually afford to cut back on paid work while you focus on your writing, or have to make the time in some other way.

When you sell your first manuscript (note, we're going with "when" not "if", and remember, it may be the third manuscript or fifth manuscript you write), look at easing back your day job so you can fit in all the business of being an author.

We heartily recommend you do not quit your day job the minute you sign your first contract. Why? Because financial pressure can eat away at your creativity.

Working outside your own writing business, even just one or two days a week, has two great benefits. First, it gives you the freedom of knowing the bills are paid. Second, it feeds into the maelstrom that is the creative mind.

Remember we talked about the importance of thinking, observing, listening and experiencing for keeping ideas flowing and your creativity alive? These things are more easily achieved if you leave the house every day for a workplace, rather than sitting at home stressing about whether your manuscript is going to be a bestseller and solve your financial woes.

The next steps: jumping off from writing

If you want "writer" to be the sole title on your business card, now's the time to get serious about marketing your business. That's right, business. You're an author. You have a book. You need to market yourself.

And when we say "now", we mean right now. Today. Not "now the first book is published". Not "now I've decided to pitch my first article".

When someone tells us they're writing their first manuscript or they're ready to set up as a freelancer, one of the first questions Val asks them is this: have you secured your website URL?

Mostly, she gets shocked looks. "Isn't that putting the cart before the horse?" the writers will ask.

The fact is that building your profile is an integral part of making a living as a writer of any kind. As a freelance writer, a profile will help you to create opportunities for yourself. And this means you need a presence online from day one.

As an author, you need to create a community around you and your work long before you sign your first book deal. Launch day for your new book should never be the first time people have heard of you. What you want is a group of excited potential readers salivating at the chance to get hold of a copy of your work.

How do you do this? The truth is that this is such a huge question that Allison created a course for the Australian Writers' Centre with a step-by-step guide on building your author platform. But, to break it down, we see that there are five pillars to successfully marketing yourself as a writer:

1. Your mindset
2. Being findable
3. Connecting with your audience online
4. Connecting with your audience in real life
5. Being practical

Let's take a brief look at each of these.

Your mindset

For many aspiring and new writers, one of the most difficult aspects to embrace about being a professional writer is the idea that writing is a business. For most of us, writing is a dream career. The notion that you could possibly put words, thoughts and ideas into the same category as nuts, bolts and potatoes is very hard to get to grips with.

But if you want to make a living as a writer in any capacity, you need to also understand that you need to sell your words, either as a product (in book form) or as a service (creating articles, newsletters, blog posts and other content for businesses).

If you were in the business of selling nuts, bolts or potatoes, you'd spread the word about your product. You'd advertise and promote them. You'd market your business. If you didn't do this, your small business wouldn't last long.

The same is true of your work as a writer. To sell your words, you need to market your words.

Fortunately, as writers today, we have so many tools at our disposal to market ourselves and our work that it needn't even feel like promotion.

But that doesn't mean you don't have to do it.

The first step in building your career as a writer, in making a living from your writing, is to get yourself in the position of having something to sell. Learn your craft, line up your ideas, learn to pitch, write your manuscript or your first articles.

The writing always comes first.

But be ready to build your profile at the same time. Push away thoughts of "self-promotion" and think instead about making connections, building a community and using your words to sell your words.

And the time to start is today.

Being findable

In the modern age, it's a truth universally acknowledged that the first thing an editor, agent, prospective client or interested party of any kind will do upon hearing your name is to Google you. If said interested party was to do that with your name today, what would they find?

In an ideal world, they'd come across YOUR website. Your website is the only place on the internet where you get to control what's written about you. It's where you get to set the tone, the message and the impact.

If you haven't yet registered your domain name – and this should be yourname.com (as in, insert *your* name not that actual URL) – do it today. And, as Valerie points out, do it within an hour of searching to see if your name is available as a URL, because she's noticed a trend where seemingly unscrupulous "investors" will buy up a URL she's just searched for. So don't search amandajones.com today and think, "I'll buy that next week." Do it now.

Remember, you don't need to have a website ready to go to register your URL. You can buy it today and simply own it for very little outlay. Then, when you know exactly what you want on your site, you're good to go.

If you can't register yourname.com or yourname.com.au or the version local to your country, then try yournameauthor.com or yournamewriter.com or yournamebooks.com or another logical variation.

Right, now that you have your URL, it's time to consider the content for your website. It needs three key sections – and these can all be on one page when you're starting out:

1. Home

The home page should tell people, at a glance, exactly where they've landed when they arrive at your site.

Allison's home page (allisontait.com) lets you know straight away that she's the author of children's adventure series fiction. Valerie's (valeriekhoo.com) tells you she's an artist, curator and storyteller.

2. About

Allison will tell you that the "about" section on her site is a consistent top 10 performer for page visits. Given that she has a deep site, containing 10 years' worth of blog content and other material, that's no mean feat.

New visitors to your website will always want to know who you are. Editors and agents will want to know about your career to date. Potential interviewers will be looking for a short, sharp bio they can use in a story or for a radio or podcast interview (Valerie and Allison will both vouch for this). Make this page work hard for you.

Your author or writer bio should always be in the third person ("Allison is the author of…" rather than "I'm the author of…"). It should start with the most recent information (that is, it's not chronological, it needs to be relevant) and you need to think of this as a selling tool, not basic information.

Allison's tip: get someone else to write your bio for you. They'll always be able to talk about you in a far more exciting way than you're willing to talk about yourself.

3. Contact

This would seem to be a no-brainer, but you'd be amazed at how many writers do not offer visitors to their site a way to contact them. You can use a contact form if you don't want to list your email address, but please make it easy for people to get in touch.

Once you're published, whether it be in book or article form, create a new page for that. Ensure that you have links to where people can view *and* buy your work.

Connecting with your audience online

Finding your audience online comes down to two things that are inextricably intertwined:

1. What are you writing?
2. Who are you trying to reach?

The internet is a vast and populous place and the key to building your profile as a writer is to find your people. If you're writing children's fiction, for instance, you need to connect with parents, teachers, librarians, booksellers, other writers, bloggers and industry professionals.

Writers of adult fiction will be searching for reviewers, bloggers, readers, editors, agents, publishers and other industry professionals.

For features writing, you'll be looking for editors, publications (so you can keep abreast of trends and interests), other writers, industry professionals and thought leaders (for story ideas), and that's just for starters.

Where do you find them? Well, they tend to flock onto various social media platforms, such as Twitter, Facebook and Instagram.

As a basic overview, Twitter tends to be the domain of writers, reviewers, bloggers, celebrities, publishing industry professionals and thought leaders. Go here for information and opinions (LOTS of opinions).

Facebook, with more than 1.74 billion users, has something for everyone. Parents are here, often in groups or following parenting websites. Readers are here – look for book clubs and the like. Writers are here, again clustered in groups or around pages such as the Australian Writers' Centre.

The main thing to remember with Facebook is that manners count – don't join a Facebook community with the sole purpose of promoting your book. Be a good community member and your profile will rise accordingly within a group of interested people.

Instagram is visual and the platform of choice for YA readers. There are a lot of readers using Instagram as a place to share short reviews and to look for recommendations. Think about how you'll present your brand before you begin here – Allison suggests coming up with five or six different areas of your writer life that you're happy to share, and then focusing on those.

As an example, her Instagram feed is full of news about her books (and other people's), her dog Procrastipup, her garden, the *So You Want To Be A Writer* podcast, and her author visits and events.

We'd need a whole separate book to really get into the ins and outs of using each of these platforms, so the best advice we can offer for beginners is to choose just one and experiment with it.

Choose the platform you think you'll be most comfortable with, and give it a bit of time. For example, Twitter can seem like a very noisy party when you first arrive, but if you choose a handful of people to follow, you'll soon learn that when it's done best, it's about one-on-one conversations. (Hint: other writers who seem to be using Twitter well are a good place to start when you're choosing who to follow.)

Remember that to get the most out of any platform, good citizenship is essential. Don't forget the "social" in social media, so engage with (and share) updates and information from other users. It's not all about you!

Connecting with your audience in real life

Many of us become writers because we like the solitude and thoughtfulness of the written word. Take us out of that zone and we get a bit twitchy.

Unfortunately, you're going to need to break through that twitch if you want to build your profile as a writer.

The easiest way to make connections in real life is simply to join an association that specialises in your area of writing. There are so many out there, and most have regular meetings or conferences. The joy of attending such events is the singular pleasure of finding yourself surrounded by writers who are talking about nothing but writing and who understand your dream to be a writer.

But a great by-product is that they then know who you are and can recommend you and your book to their audience. Just remember that it's quid pro quo. If they support you, make sure you support them in return.

Plus, it's these connections that will lead to speaking gigs at events and writers' festivals where you can get in front of your audience.

So do some research (hint, social media platforms are a great place to find out what might be happening in your local area – just ask others in your community), take a deep breath and get yourself along to an event. We always suggest that you start local, and then, perhaps, branch out from there. Genre, market or industry-specific conferences are also a brilliant way to immerse yourself in your new writing world.

Being practical

The first thing to realise on a practical level when you embark on this process is that it will not happen overnight. Building a profile takes time, which is why we suggest you get going today. The good news, though, is that you don't need to spend a lot of time on it.

For instance, people often tell us they don't have time to be on social media. And to this Valerie replies, "What? You don't have 10 minutes a day?" The truth is that while social media platforms can be black holes that drain hours from your day, they don't have to be.

Remember that you're there for a purpose. That it's part of your marketing strategy, not your entire life. That the writing always comes first.

With those things in mind, set aside the time you need. Remember the routine we talked about in the "how to be creative when you're tired" chapter, and the "make time to write" chapter? Well, add this to your routine.

It's true that in the early days, when you're setting up and getting started, you'll need longer. But once you have your accounts up and running, it shouldn't take more than 10 or so minutes a day.

Allison's top tip for not losing control of your time on social media?

Don't overthink it.

"Too many people will spend hours agonising over what to post," she says. "Don't be those people. Remember that you're out there to be you – the best possible version of you, but you nonetheless. So ask yourself, 'What am I thinking? What am I feeling? What's interesting me today?' and go with that.

"Always check your posts for spelling and grammar, make sure pictures work really well and, if you've got nothing of interest to say yourself, share someone else's post."

Aim to post once a day, and mix up the kinds of content you're sharing. A post can be as simple as a photo or as complex as a mini blog post.

Again, if you're not sure, find other authors on your social media platform of choice and really analyse what they're doing. When you find one that you think is doing a great job, copy their style (not their posts, but the kinds of content they're sharing).

Now that you're out there

Once you have your website up, your first freelance articles in print (or online) or your book published, your small business can really take off – if you're ready.

Be proactive about finding new opportunities to talk about your work with paid speaking engagements. Children's authors can make a healthy second income through creating entertaining and engaging presentations and workshops for schools, and there are several speakers' agencies in Australia to help facilitate that (see Speakers Ink, Booked Out, Lateral Learning and the Children's Bookshop Speakers' Agency as a starting point).

Authors writing for adults should investigate library talks and work on building their profile to catch the eye of festival and conference organisers. Your publisher will also pitch you for events, so make sure they know you're willing. If you lack confidence in this area, work with a public speaking coach or someone similar to build your skills.

The business of freelance writing

Much of the advice we've discussed applies to freelance writers as well. If you're strategic about your decisions and ensure you have a good mix of different clients and types of writing, you can generate a very healthy income from freelance writing. And you get paid a lot faster than having to wait for a royalty cheque from your publisher every six months!

Remember, some people don't even leave their day jobs. Instead, they freelance part-time, supplementing their main line of work with an additional revenue stream.

If getting into the world of freelancing, pitching stories to editors and finding new clients seems daunting, rest assured that momentum builds once you get started. The key is to get started!

When you begin freelancing, you need to approach editors and look for work. As you do more of it and get to know more editors, you'll find that occasionally they'll come to you with an article idea. They do this because now they know, like and trust you.

As time goes on, you'll get to a stage where you're pitching 50 per cent of the time and the other 50 per cent of the time, the work comes to you. At some point after that, you'll get to the stage of the experienced freelancer where you don't have to pitch much at all, because the work comes in the door. That corny saying is true: it won't happen overnight, but it will happen.

Set targets for yourself

It can be useful to set targets for yourself. Remember, if you're serious about making money from your writing, you need to treat it like a business.

These targets might be:

- number of pitches you send each week
- number of stories commissioned each month
- total amount invoiced each month

Do what works for you.

Valerie says, "When I first started freelancing, I decided on the yearly income I wanted to achieve. I then divided this amount by 12 to see how much I had to aim for each month in order to reach my goal."

Create a spreadsheet so you can keep track of whether you're achieving your targets. You want an easy-to-view snapshot so you can see who you've pitched to and what income is coming in. If you're on track, go celebrate! If you're not, you'll know you have to approach more editors or get more clients.

New freelance writers should actively seek new clients. Let people know you're a writer, and let them know if you have any special areas of expertise. And by "people", we mean everyone from former work colleagues to other parents at the school gate and old friends on Facebook.

Apart from getting more work, there are a couple of other factors that are vital if you want repeat business:

- **Be reliable**. Make sure you deliver when you say you'll deliver. You could be the best writer in the world, but that won't matter at all if you can't meet your deadlines. When an editor knows you're a stickler for deadlines, they'll come back to you again and again. They know you'll deliver on your promise and that they can rely on you to get the words on the page or online in time.

- **Are you positioning yourself as a freelance writer?** Is this in your bio? Is it in your email signature? We often meet people who complain they're not getting traction with their freelance writing work. They say they never get any enquiries and they're constantly pitching ideas to editors. So we look at their bio – which might be on their website or Twitter profile. And it says, "Mother. Coffee Lover. Addicted to green smoothies."

There's nothing that says "freelance writer". How can you expect other people to perceive you as a freelance writer if you don't actually tell people?! You need to position yourself as one. If you're serious about being a freelance writer, then take it seriously. Make sure it's in your bio on your website (if you have one), Twitter profile, LinkedIn and other social media.

Take an active interest in your finances

Talk to your accountant about the kinds of deductions you can make (and those you can't), and make an effort to keep records about your pitches, submissions, contracts and payments.

Many writers throw their hands up at the idea of having to keep track of the business side of their careers, and if that's you, then acknowledge it and get someone to help you. Just because you're a great writer doesn't mean you're going to be effective in all areas of your business, and that's okay – just make sure you don't ignore it.

If bookkeeping really isn't your thing, pay an expert – or, if finances won't allow that, see if you can find a numbers person who's willing to trade half a day of their core business for half a day of your writing expertise.

However, if you're fine with all of this, then celebrate – and in a big way, not an Allison "undercelebrator" way. You're in the business of writing.

CHAPTER 13

Don't just take our word for it

If there's one thing we both agree on, it's this: one of the best things about putting out the *So You Want To Be A Writer* podcast is the writing masterclass it's given us.

Over the years we've interviewed hundreds of writers about writing. We've talked to authors from every genre you can think of, from crime, romance and fantasy to literary fiction and more.

We've spoken to authors who write novels for children, for young adults and for adults, and to those who write memoir and non-fiction. We've interrogated publishers, editors, and agents who work across all different aspects of the industry.

We've also talked to freelance writers, journalists, copywriters and content writers.

Having learnt something from each and every one of them, we've pulled together some of their best tips and advice into one chapter – just for you.

Asked for their top three writing tips, most authors will offer "read widely", "be persistent" and "write, write, write". There are solid reasons why these are the most common tips – they're true, and they work.

But what you'll find here goes beyond that, into the truth about writing advice, the inside story on writing processes, industry tips from professionals, and the nitty gritty of writing your book.

This is advice taken directly from our interviews, from authors such as Charlotte Wood, Liane Moriarty, Michael Robotham, Jane Harper, Garry Disher, Hannah Kent, Veronica Roth, Graeme Simsion, Andy Griffiths, Amie Kaufman and more. From freelance writers and content writers, children's authors and crime authors, corporate writers and literary authors – almost every kind of writer you can think of.

In fact, there are more than 155 tips here from 120-plus writers.

We've edited these quotes for readability, but we've put the podcast episode number with each tip so you can listen to the entire interview if something really makes you sit up and take notice. And we've divided them into sections – one for those focussed on writing books (mostly fiction), and one for freelance writers.

Enjoy!

For writers of books

One thing you'll note as you read through the different tips here is that some of them are contradictory. To us, this is important because it demonstrates one overriding factor when it comes to writing – you. No-one will ever write in quite the same way that you do. No-one will ever approach writing a book the way that you do.

And the only way to discover how *you* write a book is to write one. To assess what works for you and what doesn't. To take on some bits of advice, but not others. To learn from the process of writing so you'll have a better idea of what you're doing next time.

The truth about writing is that it's an individual experience built on a foundation of craft and knowledge. So learn what you can and then apply it in the way that only you can.

On good and bad writing advice

When you want to become a writer, you'll hear lots of advice from all over the place. The key is to listen to people who are where you want to be one day. So if your uncle gives you advice on the creative process but all he's written are a few blog posts he's proud of, take his tips with a grain of salt.

We mean no offence to Uncle Bob, but the world of writing can be hard to navigate if you get bad or conflicting advice. Heed the counsel of people who are already where you want to be. Seek out a writers' centre whose sole aim is to help you carve a pathway in your new vocation. And listen to the advice of these authors who've shared their tips so generously to help you on your path.

Robyn Cadwallader, author, episode 233

"Be really wary of advice. There are just so many people out there who will say you can't be a writer unless you do this or do that. I'm not saying that there isn't good advice, but pick and choose where you take your advice from. And be wary of the absolutes – absolutes will tie you down."

Garry Disher, crime, young adult and literary author, episode 196

"Don't talk about writing: write. Even if you don't feel like writing, even if it's junk. The actual act of writing unlocks more words, unlocks your brain, gets the words flowing eventually."

Alan Baxter, urban fantasy author, episode 120

"Possibly one of the most damaging pieces of advice that keeps getting perpetuated is, 'If you want to be a writer you have to write every day.' I think that's bollocks, and it's really dangerous, because it makes people feel inadequate.

"I've got seven published novels and 70-something short stories. I get it done. But I absolutely don't write every day. I just can't. I've got a son to look after, I've got a business to run and that's the case for a lot of people.

"But you do have to be a writer every day in your head. If you let it drift and you just don't think about it for a couple of weeks, then you get out of that groove and you have to question where your passion really is for it.

"Even though I absolutely can't write every day, I'm always in the mindset of a writer. You see things and you observe people, and you look at situations and you always take those in with that writerly mind and subconsciously think about what you can use. I'll regularly be turning over ideas for a story in my head."

Allison Rushby, children's and YA author, episode 4

"I really hate hearing other writers say, 'You must write every day and you must write your 10 pages.' Well, I've got two kids, a husband and a cat, you know? I can't write every day. That's just not how life works. It's not how publishing works, either. Some months I don't have time to write anything because I'm editing. Or speaking.

"For me, and I think for lots of writers, the creative process can't be set in stone like this. You don't need to write every day and certainly not a set amount. Life happens and there's no point feeling guilty about it. If you can manage to keep writing and keep squeezing it in where you can and inching forward with those words, then that's what really matters."

What should you write?

You know you want to be a writer, but you're not sure what to write about. It could be because of the terror of the blank page. You could be paralysed by the idea that you might not be able to produce the goods. Or you might actually have so many ideas flying around that you simply can't pick which one to focus on.

Here, our author friends share their thoughts on how to decide what to write about.

Deborah Abela, children's author, episode 235

"Put your heart in front. Go with that idea you love. Of course, what you love may not be what a publisher thinks they can sell, what the sales departments think will sell in bulk. But it's really, really important to be led by your heart.

"I've seen too many authors along the way say, 'I'm going to write this book because these are really selling right now.' And it doesn't work, because their heart's not with them.

"I've seen other authors go, 'You know what? I don't know if this will sell, but I really, desperately want to write this story.' In some cases, it's been their most successful work. And it's because the reader can almost hear their beating heart as they turn the pages."

Josephine Moon, author, episode 231

"The adage goes, 'Write what you know.' That's a good place to start and it will get you so far. But I always say to people, 'Write what you *want* to know.' Because that really engages your curiosity and gives you that freshness of looking at something with keen new eyes, rather than something that's maybe a bit stagnant, that you already know. It's a forward momentum.

"Write short stories. Just keep writing short stories. And deliberately write in a whole heap of different genres. So write a mystery, write a romance, write a crime, write a children's story – whatever it is. Just keep changing genres so you find your voice and your niche.

"A short story is not a massive commitment. Putting out a 2000 or 3000-word short story, sometimes you can do that in a day. Certainly within a week. It's not a huge commitment, but you'll get a lot of value back from it."

Deborah Rodriguez, author, episode 210

"It's really important that, no matter what, you stay true to your craft. Writing is very artistic – it's an art form. You're painting a beautiful canvas of a story. You want the book to sell, but you need to focus on your craft, and you need to take the time to get to know your characters. Think about the book as a piece of art rather than a money maker."

Jacqueline Harvey, children's author, episode 198

"You need to work out who you want to be as a writer. What sort of stories do you love the most? For me, it was about realising that when I write a story, I'm nine years old. That's my part of the world."

Louise Park, children's author and series concept creator, episode 189

"If you want to write, know who you're writing for. Know that audience. Get in there and be with them. It's not enough just to think, 'I want to write for 10-year-olds and I remember what being a 10-year-old was like.' That won't cut it. You need to get in among them. Share your writing with them in the developing phases and get their feedback.

"They're going to be your toughest critics, and you want them to be addicted to your books and waiting for the next one to come out. The best way to know you're hitting the mark is to hear directly from the horse's mouth. So know who your target market is.

"Then, go into shops – anywhere that stocks books – and look. Look for your competition, observe what they're doing right, see where there's a gap, and go for that gap. Try to fill that gap."

James Bradley, author, episode 239

"Write the thing you want to read. All of that stuff about trying to guess what the market wants, trying to guess what publishers want, trying to guess what agents want, is not the way to write a book. First of all, it's not the way to write a good book. But it's also not the way to write a book you want to write. The rewards of writing a book are not great in financial terms. So you should write the book you actually want to write. And then work out what to do with it."

Di Morrissey, commercial fiction author, episode 254

"Write what interests you. They say write about what you know about, which is all very well. But I don't want to know how the back of a computer works or whatever happens to be your specialty.

"So write about things that you feel passionate about, that you're really concerned about or that you love. Write about what touches you and what interests you."

Sophie Green, publisher and commercial fiction author, episode 194

"I needed to write something that was meaningful to me, because readers can always tell when something is done cynically. But, also, I did look around and think, 'Where is the big landscape book?'

"By big, I mean it's about big themes and is not shy of being ambitious as well. That's something I've long thought about and talked about with other writers – being ambitious. Be ambitious for a big readership, be ambitious for the scope of the story, be ambitious about the themes and emotions you're addressing."

Zanni Louise, children's author, episode 169

"Constantly keep an ear out or an eye out for ideas. Every little moment in your life can become something bigger, and can become a story. It can become a fiction series. There's so much opportunity and so many ideas. It's about just attending to them."

Carole Wilkinson, children's author, episode 158

"Don't say no. I'd never have come to writing children's fiction if I hadn't said, 'Yes, I will do fiction as an elective,' or 'Yes, I will write a teen novel, even though it has never occurred to me in my whole life.' I've said yes to a lot of things that didn't work out – for instance, I wrote for a couple of kids' TV series, which was a disaster, but it was good to know about that.

"Rather than sitting and waiting for something to happen, you've got to make stuff happen. And anything you write – even the brochures and educational handbooks that I wrote – everything will teach you something about writing or publishing. And you meet people. I met my publisher through doing other things.

"Leave yourself open, because you don't always know what it is you should be writing."

Tania McCartney, children's author and illustrator, episode 150

"Stop worrying about filling a market niche or a gap or this amazing idea you've had that's going to blow everyone out of the water and make you millions – and instead, listen to your heart. Write from your heart.

"Yes, learn how writing is done, learn about plot, learn about character development, all that technical stuff, yes. But then write from your heart, and write what you love and what you're passionate about. Because that provides authenticity.

"Publishers want authenticity. And your readers – whether they're two or 102 – want authenticity in what they're reading, so they can feel connected, emotionally secured in the book, and want to read more from you. So just write your passion and what you love."

Oliver Phommavanh, children's author, episode 144

"Try not to take it too seriously. Especially with kids writing. Kids are not reading all the time. They're also playing, they're also mucking around. So the best way to get into kids' writing is to try to get into that aspect as well.

"Do a bit of writing, be serious for some of the time, but other times just play and have fun. I find that if you're not having fun, there's a great chance that the kids aren't going to have fun with the book, either. There needs to be a sense of playfulness with your writing, no matter what genre you're writing."

Hannah Kent, author, episode 137

"Don't wait until you're ready. We rarely feel ready for anything in this life, particularly creative projects like writing, because we're operating in an atmosphere of uncertainty. That's what makes it original.

"You have no guiding light, you have no sense of how it's all going to turn out. It's mysterious, but that can often mean that we don't really know where to begin.

"So the best thing to do is just begin. Just start. Don't wait until you feel ready for it."

Meg McKinlay, children's author, episode 103

"Let yourself be your absolute strangest self, because we're all fundamentally strange and weird at heart. And those little connections we make, we'll make them in a way that no-one else can. I really think that's where the most interesting stories and ideas come from."

Lindsey Kelk, author, episode 63

"Always be listening, because there are stories everywhere. I hear so many people say to me, 'I'd love to write, but I don't know what to write about.' There's no point in trying to write if you don't have a story to tell, because every page will be painful if you're trying to force something that doesn't exist.

"But there are stories in every conversation you have. In every human you interact with, there's a story. So always be listening and always be paying attention."

Nick Earls, author, episode 28

"Value small ideas when you have them and don't lose them. In my case that means writing them down on scraps of paper, or if I don't have a scrap of paper I'll put them on my phone."

Anita Heiss, author, episode 2

"It's really important for writers to know why they're writing. To sit down and go, 'Why do I want to write this book? Why do I want this book out? What's its purpose? What's the goal?' That will help to determine and harness their motivation and their determination to finish their project."

Learning the craft
Bren Macdibble/Cally Black, children's and YA author, episode 272

"Pick apart the things you love and look for techniques. Follow those authors and read everything that they write about how they write and how they think they're achieving what they want to achieve. Then go back and pick apart their work again. Because you can learn a lot by just stalking the authors you love and picking apart their techniques."

Sarah Bailey, crime author, episode 215

"Do a course. Cherry pick a couple of courses that really will kickstart your interest in writing, or a particular topic you get stuck on. For me, a basic creative writing course was so helpful. Just that re-programming I needed to do with structure and the character journey really helped me think about my stories in a more scientific way. When you're writing crime, that's really helpful because there's such a structure to it."

Shankari Chandran, thriller author, episode 200

"I wish I'd done a course months before I started on the project. It gave me enormous skills, tools and awareness, and the confidence to look at my work, to see what I'd done, to not be afraid of deconstructing it and rewriting it. And to really enjoy that process.

"Also to see the conventions of the genre not as a burden or requirements that you must meet, but as this wonderful set of guidelines that you'd enjoy aspiring to and meeting."

Margaret Morgan, author, episode 251

"Doing a course allowed me to get feedback from other people. It made a big difference. I learnt about pacing, structure, characterisation, point of view and voice. Those sorts of things are the real craft issues."

Catherine Pelosi, children's author, episode 222

"When I did a course, I met other writers and it opened that door into a community I just haven't left since. I try to attend a lot of conferences. Even just getting involved online – on social media – there's a big publishing industry presence on Twitter and that sort of thing. It was like going through a door into another world."

Fleur Ferris, YA and middle-grade author, episode 122

"I was doing a course and when you write something and you know somebody is going to be reading it – your peers as well as your instructor – it gives you confidence and lets you know where you sit. That gave me the confidence and courage to actually approach an agent. Doing that course put me in the right place to submit my work."

The writing process

The writing process – like most creative processes – is a magical thing.

Sometimes it's very process driven and you can clearly see the output you're going to get at the end of it.

At other times it's more organic, and that's when you'll need to rely on a unique combination of your skills, experiences, creativity and inspiration in order to produce something that completely surprises everyone, including yourself.

Here, our fabulous authors share their tips on how you can wrangle, harness and leverage the writing process to your advantage.

Dervla McTiernan, crime author, episode 271
"Don't believe too much in the myth of the whole 'messy first draft'. I think it's true that you should feel free to have a very messy first draft. But I think you can make it really hard for yourself if it's completely stream-of-consciousness stuff. At the end of the day, you are writing a novel, or non-fiction if that's what you're writing, and I think that just having some structure to that first draft can be helpful. That's not for everybody, but that's my approach."

Anna Snoekstra, crime author, episode 244
"Don't try to write something good. This sounds counterproductive, but it's really important when you write something, especially when you're first starting out, to not be too focused on whether it's good or not.

"There should be so many more things in your head before that. Is it saying what I want it to say? Why am I trying to tell this story?

What kind of hole is it trying to fill? Ask yourself these questions, rather than, 'Is it good?'

"If you're too afraid of it being good or bad, it can almost stop you writing, because there's that fear about other people's opinions even as you're just trying to tell the story you want to tell.

"Try not to have too much fear when you're writing. Because the things that are really exciting, that new writers are writing, are things that push boundaries and tackle a subject that other people haven't tackled in that way before.

"So write your truth and write without fear, which can be really hard. But if you're scared to write it, often it's something that really needs to be written."

Sally Hepworth, author, episode 223

"Don't be afraid to write badly. Sometimes perfectionism can be our worst enemy. My first drafts usually resemble a dog's breakfast. I wouldn't even show them to my dog. But I get the book down fast, and I get that idea out. So don't worry about finding the perfect phrase, and just get that story down. Because ultimately that's what we're doing – we're telling stories.

"Write fast. This is not for everyone – some people prefer to write slowly. But I've found that the faster I write, and the more I focus on moving forward, then the better I write, the better I keep a handle on what the story is.

"Stories can become quite bulky. If we slow down too much we can start going off on tangents, because we don't have that fluid movement. You can always go back and fill things out later, once you know how it ends and where you need more. But for me, writing fast really propels the story forward and creates a better, tighter story."

Jackie French, author, episode 214

"Always, always break narrative expectations – that is, what the reader expects. You need to break reader expectation with every plot device and every character.

"This is important in novels, but it's especially necessary in picture books where you need tension on every page. Every time you turn a page in a picture book, the reader cannot know what's going to happen next.

"No-one has ever turned pages to say, 'Oh isn't that lovely description, I'm going to turn the page to get more description.' They turn the page because you've created a world they don't want to leave, and to find out what happens next. If they can predict what's happening, then you've failed as a writer."

Kate Forsyth, author, episode 204

"Understand that your story has an engine. The story is like a machine, and it's driving somewhere. Know that you need to create that engine. Something has to happen to move your plot forward on every single page of your story. If I could just teach that to everybody, we'd see a lot less bad writing."

Garry Disher, author, episode 196

"When I'm describing a place or a person, in subtle ways I try to evoke one or more of the senses. But I'm also thinking, 'Get in, get out, don't linger.' That's one of the lessons the famous author Raymond Carver tried to convey. Get in, get out, don't linger. So when you do get in, it has to be as clear and evocative and as succinct as possible."

Patti Miller, memoirist and teacher, episode 191

"Journal writing is a really useful thing to do as a writer, for all sorts of reasons. But, and I don't mean to sound rude, writing in a journal is a little bit like throwing up. You need to do it, but you don't do it in public. Or you *try* not to do it in public, at least. This is the kind of writing that helps you sort through stuff.

"When you're writing for others to read, you're constructing a world for them to inhabit. And so you look at the craft of it. You look at the craft of how you build that world. So I always remind writers, 'You're building a world for other people when you write.'"

Belinda Castles, author, episode 238

"If you can, you should walk or swim. It will help you think. Little problems will just get solved when you walk away from them and do some exercise. As far as is physically possible for people, if you can find the exercise that suits you when you're writing, it's like magic."

Matthew Benns, journalist and non-fiction author, episode 187

"I feel so strongly with writing, having done it for so long, and particularly as a tabloid journalist, that one word can convey so much emotion. And the way you feel as you write comes through.

"If I'm laughing when I'm writing, it's like my laughter comes through the words and hits the reader, and they start laughing too. I don't know how that happens. Because you read the words individually and you think, 'Well, they're actually not that funny.' But you watch people read them and they're smiling."

Jane Harper, crime author, episode 265

"In terms of the actual execution, a lot of writing a crime novel is about thinking really hard about how you're going to let the information unfold. At what points are you going to give the readers certain knowledge that they need – and how will you drip-feed that?

"You can't leave it all to the end and you can't pile it all in at the start. You've got to give little rewards, things that keep people engaged and give them a bit more information to push the story forward without giving it all away too quickly. Or making them wait too long either, because that's equally frustrating.

"Get people interested early. You can't spend a lot of time expecting people will stick with you for some sort of promised reward at the end. You've got to engage them right from the start. You've got to keep them engaged throughout.

"When I was doing my journalism training, we were always told to assume people wouldn't finish our articles. They'll get bored, they'll get distracted, and you've got to try to keep them in there. And that's what I think when I'm writing the books. What can I do to get them to turn one more page and just keep on going? And to stick with it right to the end."

Fiona McIntosh, commercial fiction author, episode 264

"You must write forwards all the time. Don't keep reading what you wrote yesterday. Because what you wrote yesterday is the fastest way for you to get trapped in a horrible abyss of editing at the time when you shouldn't be editing.

"When you're writing, you should be wearing your writer's cap and just go forwards. All the time. Don't look back. Just go forwards. And then, later, pull that cap off and put your editing cap on and then look at the story as a whole. Look at the whole architecture of the story. And then you've got a much better idea of what the story looks like, feels like, sounds like."

Karen Foxlee, children's author, episode 257
"Novels are made from sentences, and you just have to lay them down. It might feel like you're getting nowhere, but you will get somewhere."

Joanna Nell, author, episode 256
"This is a tip I'm going to call '20 options', to try to get over either writer's block or anything you're having trouble with in your writing.

"It's a tip I learnt from Australian author Valerie Parv, who's been very generous to aspiring writers, a very generous mentor.

"What she suggests is that if you're coming up against a problem – it might be the name of a character, you're not sure where to set it, this person might have a super power but you don't know what it is, they might have a special pet, you've got your characters into a predicament and don't know how to escape – then get a piece of paper and write the numbers one to 20 down the side.

"Then, next to each one, put in a potential solution, a potential option. And just brainstorm. It doesn't matter if they're outlandish or ridiculous. I can almost guarantee that by the time you've got to 20, the answer will be there staring you in the face."

Jaclyn Moriarty, adult, YA and children's author, episode 209
"People always say, 'Keep a diary.' I never found that very helpful until I started a different kind of diary, which is a kind of stream of consciousness thing that I write most days.

"I try to write on my computer so I can write it fast. I try to each day write, not just a description of what happened that day, but a few lines where I talk about the details of one incident from my day, or one conversation I had, or describe one person I met. Or I try to get underneath one emotion that I had, try to explore it. It really helps with character descriptions."

Tristan Bancks, children's and YA author, episode 201

"I write a lot of drafts over a very long period of time. The first draft is terrible – the pacing is all over the place, and it shoots off in a million different directions. And then, with the second and the third and the fourth, the pacing is still all out. I either deliver too much information right up front, and you know exactly what's going on, or I make it too cryptic and no-one knows what's going on.

"So I keep all those drafts to myself until I get to about a fifth or sixth draft. These are drafts that sometimes will take up to four months or five months or something to write the 50,000-word draft."

Jacqueline Harvey, children's author, episode 198

"I'm a planner. I sit and plan out the big ideas for the story, so I know the major plot twists and turns. And I always start with a good idea of the ending, because I don't like surging towards nothing.

"And for me, because I can tend to overwrite 10,000 words, I'd rather not if I don't have to. So I plan, and I edit as I go."

Garry Disher, crime, YA, literary author, episode 196

"I think I've developed techniques as a crime writer that can enrich fiction writing for anybody. For example, carefully placed turning points, buried secrets coming to the surface, getting the reader to exercise their mind about the wrong issue, delaying and withholding tactics.

"The reader badly wants to know, but your job as a writer, and as a crime writer, is to not satisfy that need. Partial and doubtful outcomes, and that sort of thing – they're techniques I've learnt as a crime writer and they've enriched my other types of fiction.

"Also, I love a quote from Charles Dickens. He said, 'Make them laugh, make them cry, but crucially make them wait.' In other words, you string the reader along. You don't spell it all out."

Sophie Green, publisher and commercial fiction author, episode 194

"Every sentence has to advance the story. That's a very hard discipline, but it's a crucial one. It doesn't mean everything's quick in a story. It just means looking at every sentence you're writing and thinking, 'Is that necessary? Am I wasting someone's time by putting in that detail? Is that something that only I should know as the author but the characters can't know, or the narrator can't know?'

"You need to deliver information to the reader when they need it, as they need it, no more and no less, and you need to keep that story moving forward.

"If you can keep those rules in mind, you're always serving the reader and serving the story. That's how you can keep it entertaining.

"It's when things drag, or when you think you can go off on a little indulgence as a writer, and maybe engage in a scene that doesn't really do anything much and doesn't serve the characters and doesn't serve the characters' stories – that's when it's not entertaining. That's when readers can feel like maybe they don't want to proceed with this story, or maybe they lose interest altogether."

Hilary Spiers, author, episode 154

"Some of my best ideas come when I'm either just about to fall asleep or maybe I wake in the night and I've just got an idea and it's floating around. It's at those moments that I write my best prose, but I don't write it down. And the next morning when I wake up I think, 'What was that sentence? What was I going to get them to do?'

"I'd say to everybody, 'Don't do as I do. Write it down when you think of it.' It's like being out shopping and you see something and you get your notebook out and you just scribble a few words to remind yourself. You have to do it when it happens."

Andy Griffiths, children's author, episode 67

"I'm a big believer in the timed writing practice and putting the hours in. Writing for at least half an hour to an hour a day. That practice can start with just five minutes a day. That's how I started – trying to fill up two pages of an exercise book. That was my basic daily commitment. That very quickly strengthened and I found much more to write about until it was 10 minutes, 15 minutes, so you build up.

"That constant practice – not creating a story, but just exploring yourself – that's really useful."

Kate Forsyth, historical fiction author, episode 21

"I don't start writing my novel until I have it fully visualised in my mind's eye, in my imagination. I don't start writing my novel until I can hear the voice of my primary characters and the voice of the story and it's clamouring in my ear, demanding to be told. I don't start my novel until I feel utterly in control of my material and the fictional world feels real to me. That can take an awfully long time.

"My notebook is a way of chronicling my creative journey towards the novel, showing the way that I discover the story and allowing me to keep all of my research, all my ideas, all of my inspirations in the one spot so that wherever I go I can carry it with me and I look back on it and I can be reinspired and I can remember what it is that I'm trying to do."

Beatrice Colin, historical fiction author, episode 140

"Plotting's very difficult. It has to be two by two equals four. You can't have two by two equals five. So if you start off with a problem, you can't answer another one at the end. You know, she's in love with the wrong man and it's all awful, and then at the very end she discovers her mother was a nun. Something else. It has to answer the problem, otherwise it doesn't work. Quite a lot of people make that mistake and answer another question.

"There isn't the *right* plot, either. There are many plots. You just have to choose the one, or go with the one that feels right at the time. And that can change. I've had an idea for an ending, and then I've rewritten it maybe five or six times. But just knowing that I've got the ending gives me the confidence to write towards it."

Hannah Kent, author, episode 137

"I find it hard to plot without knowing my characters. So probably the first 30,000 words I write are really just introductions. Often I end up throwing out a lot of that, but it enables me to become familiar with my characters.

"Then, with that familiarity, I find I can put these characters who I know intimately into situations of conflict. The plot will unfold from there, because I know how those characters are going to react to those situations.

"From that point on, it becomes quite easy to map out a book, because I know the various things that need to happen and I can anticipate the responses my characters will have to those situations. And how those responses will lead to further situations of conflict."

Anna Spargo-Ryan, author, episode 110

"I write quite a lot in fragments. I have different scenes that will occur to me, and I write them separately. I know that later on they might show up in the book, and it's helpful, not just to get the words down, but also to understand the characters in the story better.

"Some of that stuff doesn't end up in the book, but it's still been useful in terms of understanding what the book is for and what it's about."

Anne Gracie, romance fiction author, episode 64

"Go deep and be true to the characters. Readers will follow you anywhere, as long as you're true to the characters. If you completely manipulate them and just have a character doing whatever it is you need them to do at that moment for the sake of the plot, I don't follow that.

"They're what I call 'wall bangers' – the books you start reading and then chuck against the wall because, 'Nup, she wouldn't do that! I'm sick of it.'

"If you're assuming that connection with the characters is what people like about your stories, then you've got to treat your characters with respect and let them reveal themselves."

Charlotte Wood, author, episode 39

"Be prepared to be vulnerable. When we first start writing, we tend to write things in the hope they'll make people think highly of us. Those aren't the things that are interesting, really, because there's always some sort of self-protection going on. But once you start really investigating the weird things that truly interest you, in your own strange brain, then passion wins out.

"If you follow what really interests you, you'll get to the heart of some good work, whereas if you think, 'I want to write a book like, say, Rachel Cusk,' you're simply imitating. You can't do it.

"In Annie Dillard's wonderful book *The Writing Life*, she quotes Thoreau: 'Know your own bone: gnaw at it, bury it, unearth it and gnaw at it still.' I really believe in this, especially for literary fiction. Just find what is particular to you, the thing you're fascinated by, and go there – and don't worry about what people are going to think of you for doing it."

Michael Robotham, crime author, episode 26

"The magic in the writing process is in not letting people know too much about it. You don't want to give people the plot to your latest book. Day to day you can't really tell them that much about what you're writing.

"My friends ask me all the time, 'What are you working on?' I say, 'Well, it's another book,' but I don't want to tell them too much. One of the great failings of people who want to write is that they leave all their energy out there, because they tell people about the book they want to write. They spend months or weeks or days talking about this book they want to write.

"They should spend all of that energy actually writing the thing. Don't just tell everyone and talk about it and discuss it with people. Sit down and write it."

How to get the book written

Writing a book can be daunting. There are so many words! It can sometimes seem like an endless process where you wonder if you'll ever get to type the words "The End". Apart from the challenges of writing itself, you can be pulled in so many directions, thanks to a bazillion different factors in life.

So how do you actually get your book written? These authors share what they think you need to do. All of them have written and published their books. Some have done this multiple times. So they know a thing or two about getting it done. If you're in the middle of your manuscript, with what seems like no end in sight, read on!

Eliza Henry-Jones, author, episode 224

"Recognise how you write. For a very long time, I went to a lot of writing workshops, heard a lot of authors speak, and every author I heard speak was a plotter.

"I went home and I tried to plot everything and be very, very organised and have every chapter outlined and all that sort of thing. And it's just not how my brain operates. It was like pushing a boulder up a hill. It made things really difficult.

"You need to be able to recognise how you write – whether you're the sort of person who needs to write 500 or 1000 words every day, or whether you're better off writing in a big stint once or twice a week and then letting it sit and churn away in the back of your head in between. Or whether you need to write chronologically, or whether it's better for you to just write all the scenes that jump out at you.

"Being critical, and interrogating whether how you're writing is what's best for your brain and how you operate, is really important."

Jack Heath, children's, YA and crime author, episode 221

"It's a good idea to join your local writers' centre, because they can give you advice and you can do workshops. To get better at any skill, you need training, practice and feedback. For writing, practice is easy to get, but feedback is very, very difficult. A writers' centre can be helpful with that."

Sarah Bailey, crime author, episode 215

"I set really strange little deadlines for myself all the time – whether it's that chapter, that word count, that problem I need to solve, that date that this needs to be done by. It helps me stay on track. If I didn't do it, I don't think my books would get written."

Kirsty Manning, author, episode 240

"Get some tools and learn the craft. It's really valuable to do a creative writing course, because you really learn about the craft of writing."

Pamela Hart, historical fiction author and creative writing director at the Australian Writers' Centre, episode 242

"Find your tribe. Find your community. And obviously one of the things I love about the Australian Writers' Centre is that we offer that option for people. We're a tribe, and we're a community, and we're a very welcoming one.

"Beyond that, there are possibilities of finding other tribes. They could be fiction or children's fiction or romance – there are other people out there doing the same stuff you're doing. You need to find them. It's only an internet search away."

Fiona McIntosh, commercial fiction author, episode 264

"If you write with freedom and no constraints, the power in your storytelling will emerge so much stronger. It will be full of oxygen. But if you let that whole care factor get you down, how good is it? Is it good enough? Are people going to buy this? Should I have an agent? You just want to say, 'No-one cares about this yet. So stop worrying, and just get on and write it.'"

Jane Harper, crime author, episode 265

"Aim for consistency. Find a little bit of time as often as you can and really keep those ideas and that creativity flowing.

"Work on your technical ability. People underestimate their ability to improve in a creative field. They seem to think that for some reason, whatever natural talent you have is all that you have and all you'll ever have. It's just not true. You can absolutely improve."

Kayte Nunn, historical fiction author, episode 247

"Be prepared to do the work. I've had people say to me, 'Oh, I think I'll try that.' And it's just not something you can do half-heartedly, write a book."

Louise Park, children's author and series creator, episode 189

"Have a really good writers' group that you can work with – a group of friends who want to write and keep writing. Some groups meet once a week, some groups meet once a month, but you know you've got to have a certain amount finished by that meeting.

"It's a criticism-free zone, but it's a lot of constructive advice. You read, you share, you talk it apart, you look at plot holes and fill them in. It will keep you going to get to your endgame of having something written."

Natasha Lester, historical fiction author, episode 186

"My secret goal is to convert the world to Scrivener, one writer at a time. It's actually not a secret goal – I tell everybody! It's the most amazing piece of software, and it changed my writing life when I discovered it.

"One of the reasons is the fact that you can keep all your research documents in the one place, along with your manuscript. So every photograph I take on the streets of New York goes into my Scrivener document.

"Scrivener enables you to do a couple of things with a photograph. When I'm typing my story and there's a particular location I'm writing about that I have a photo of, I can put a link in my manuscript to that picture.

"I can then click on that link and the photo will pop up, so it's right there when I'm writing. Or I can create a separate window to have it on-screen the whole time I'm writing.

"It's the same with anything I find on the internet. A PDF document with an *Atlantic Monthly* article, for example, it all goes into my Scrivener research folder. So I don't have to leave Scrivener and go to the internet and look up the article, which will then lead me on to things like Facebook and wormholes of wasted time.

"I just click on the article within Scrivener and it pops up in another window, so I can have both the article and my document open at the same time.

"It's a really great and efficient way to organise your research, to have it all there and make sure you only stay in the one program for your writing time. You never have to leave that program."

Nicole Alexander, author, episode 184
"The most efficient way of getting through the work is simply to do something every day. It doesn't matter if I only get 400 words down on the page, at least the work is present in my mind. I'm not continually having to go back and double-check things, which is how I worked in the early days. Because I'd be like, 'Oh this is fine. I can go away and do my other work for a week or 10 days and come back to it.' No, it's got to be percolating in my head all the time."

Ben Hobson, author, episode 180
"I have two young boys, and fitting in a full-time job it's often about 8.30 or 9pm that I can switch off for the day. So then I try

to cram in, honestly, probably about 30 minutes' worth of writing a day, to an hour. When I'm writing a first draft, I force myself to do 1000 words every day."

Kristel Thornell, author, episode 141

"Finding a routine that works for you is really central. Something that's doable. Don't set yourself up to feel like you're not achieving your goal. Figure out something you can actually achieve, an amount of time at a certain time of day when you know you'll be able to get that done.

"There needs to be a sense of a reliable structure that will support you, keep you in place and make sure you get something done. You also need to enjoy it as much as possible, otherwise you won't stay with it.

"The processes are so long, and you'll need so much patience, that you'll have to have something that both supports you and helps to discipline you, and that won't feel like suffering."

Hannah Kent, author, episode 137

"Trust in the process. Talent is a wonderful thing, but it doesn't count for much in the long run. What counts is showing up, having a writing routine, sitting at the desk, even for just 20 minutes a day or whatever you can manage, and working and writing when you don't feel like it. That's how books get written.

"I don't think books get written through muses, or gifts, or talent, or genius. Books get written by people who start when they're not even sure what they're going to do, who just keep showing up and keep on doing it. That's the secret."

Veronica Roth, YA author, episode 133

"It's all about having this tension of humility and self-advocacy. You have to believe in your story, but you also have to believe that it can be better. It's a weird balancing act. If you're in love with the process of writing and you're committed to being a better writer with each story you write, but you're also aware of your strengths, then you can advocate for your book without being stubborn.

"It's a nice little trial and error. I bounce back and forth like a pendulum all the time, but I do believe in my work. I also believe in myself and my capacity to get better. I try to listen to feedback, but if it doesn't resonate then I let it go."

Jay Kristoff, speculative fiction author, episode 127

"I didn't quit my day job until we sold *Illuminae*. It was a wonderful feeling, selling that first book, and the high of it kind of pushed me through, so I was able to work a day job and write. But for a while there I was essentially working two day jobs. I'd get home at night and write for three, four, five hours a night and stay up until 2am. I did that five years – I got by on five or six hours sleep every night.

"You'd be very lucky to receive an advance large enough to quit your day job on your first novel. So, unless you want to take a real financial gamble, which we weren't prepared to do, it was a matter of just finding those extra hours.

"My friends kind of forgot what I looked like and I gave up playing video games and going out to movies and whatever, and just kind of knuckled down and did this as hard as I possibly could."

John Birmingham, multi-genre writer, episode 118

"You really need to commit to a method. You can't just wander into a café and order a flat white and a muffin and wait for the muse to write your heartbreaking work of ****ing staggering genius. You need to decide, 'If I'm going to be a writer, I'm going to write. And I'm going to do it this way. I'm going to be at my desk at 8.30 in the morning and I'm going to be there until 2.30 in the afternoon.'

"You'll have your own way. It may not be the same as my way, but you have to settle on a working routine and you need to stick to it.

"Stephen King has a rule, he writes 2000 words a day, every day, that's just it. That's his rule.

"My rule is a little different, but you'll need a rule and you'll need to stick to it, because the thing about writing is that it does afford you unlimited freedom for ****ing up. And, as much as possible, you don't want to indulge that freedom."

Kimberly McCreight, YA author, episode 116

"Often people have such high standards for themselves, and they compare their work to their favourite author. They don't even want to put it on the page when it's bad. The reality is all these published books you're reading started out bad. The early drafts of everybody's books have been worse than when they're finished.

"Lower your standards for yourself so you can get something finished – no-one's going to read that early draft. That's between you and your computer. Just get it finished and then you can worry about turning it into something great."

Natasha Lester, historical fiction author, episode 106

"Write anyway. We're all capable of coming up with so many excuses to stop us from writing, but if we just sit down and write anyway then that's how we get a book written.

"It doesn't matter if we're tired or we're busy or we're not feeling well, or if we think we don't have the time, or we think, 'My writing is rubbish,' which we all often do. If we just sit down and keep writing on anyway, regardless of all of those thoughts, procrastinations and excuses, we will eventually get a book written."

Holly Seddon, thriller author, episode 92

"Setting daily targets is a big one for me – to make things bite-sized. For me, it's 1000 words a day. I'm quite a fast writer. For other people their target could be 500 words a day, and even if it's 100 it adds up. Then I'm not always looking at how huge the task is – I'm actually looking at how small the task is daily."

Nicky Pellegrino, author, episode 65

"Have a comfortable chair, because you'll be spending a lot of time sitting in it."

Pamela Hart, historical fiction author, episode 58

"I like Pat Farmer's advice: the number-one reason your book will never be published is that you haven't written it. If you want to be a writer you have to write, and you have to prioritise it.

"People say, 'Oh, I'd like to write a book, if only I had time.' If you're watching three hours of television a week, you have time to write a book."

Judith Rossell, children's author and illustrator, episode 51
"I had a student who was working as a waitress, and she would text her novel to herself on her little breaks. At the end of the day she'd collect those texts together and write another paragraph. You have to want it, and you have to be determined."

Kylie Ladd, author, episode 32
"I aim for 1000 words in a writing session. If I don't make the 1000 words, I get back on the computer when the kids are in bed and I stay there until I do. I'm very, very disciplined about that. I'm a very disciplined person, full stop. I make timetables and I stick to them, and that's the only way I find I achieve anything. I can't go to bed until the 1000 words are written, essentially."

Liane Moriarty, author, episode 25
"Writing your first novel is like being on a diet. That's why programs like Weight Watchers are so successful – you've got to have something that keeps you going. Anybody can write their first chapter, but it's a really long task to finish a novel.

"Either join a writers' group or get a friend to become a writing partner. Set up a contract with somebody, say, 'I promise I'll get you a chapter by such and such a date.' That sort of thing. You've got to trick yourself into writing the first novel."

Working with a co-author

Creating a book with someone else is a completely different experience from working on your own – it's also an area of writing that isn't often discussed, so it can be hard to find tips on the best process to use. Fortunately, it's a subject we've been able to explore through several interviews…

Ali Berg, co-author of *The Book Ninja* with Michelle Kalus, episode 241

"Constantly communicate with each other. Because, especially in the midst of it, we could get in our own heads a bit and write things and take characters places and then forget to tell one another. Then the character has completely changed and you haven't communicated.

"Even if it's an email or a Facebook message, just let each other know what's happening in your mind."

Jay Kristoff, co-author of the *Illuminae* series with Amie Kaufman, episode 127

"We plot together. We get together physically and we generally plot about 100 pages in advance. If we do more than that, we find the story will evolve and we'll think of cooler ideas. So any more than 100 pages of plotting tends to be wasted time. We'll start to trip over our own feet.

"Then we divide up those 100 pages into scenes or points of view, and we divide the writing duties based on those points of view."

Nicholas Lochel, co-author of the *Zarkora* series with his sister Alison Lochel, episode 70

"What we did at the very beginning was talk. We had months of just talking and we plotted out the entire story. We went all the way from the beginning to the end. We'd get a lot of detail into the scenes and then we broke it down into chapters, then into books.

"After that, we'd go off and write our versions of each of the books. Then I'd grab Ali's manuscript and I'd see what I liked with hers, and she'd obviously read mine and tell me what she liked. I'd then merge the two manuscripts together to make the first draft."

Getting that first publishing deal

You've written the book and now you want to see it on the shelves of your local bookstore. A few things happen before that milestone. Apart from the fact that you need to write a good book, we've already mentioned that you need to get to know the industry and connect with people.

Here's some advice from authors who've been there.

Amie Kaufman, YA and children's author, episode 276

"I always suggest to people who are querying that they don't send all their queries out at once. Send out just a handful – 10 at most if you're querying the US, where there are lots of agents, but preferably even fewer. And then wait. If you don't get requests [for full manuscripts] that doesn't speak to your manuscript, it speaks to your pitch because that's what they're reading first. If your pitch is no good, you can have the best book in the world but no one's going to read it.

"I have a couple of rules in mind when I write a pitch. The first is that it needs to follow this very basic structure: 'When [incident] happens to [character] they must [action] before [consequence]. I use that formula for every story, and if you can't fit your story in that, then it may point to a problem with your story. Second, stick to 200 words and don't give away the ending. You're not writing a synopsis. It's much better to think of your pitch as the 'back of the book copy'. You're writing the blurb."

Lesley Gibbes, children's author, episode 213

"There are not a lot of publishing houses that open up to unsolicited manuscripts; it's getting narrower and narrower. So you need to go to the festivals and book in with your manuscripts and have them looked at by editors, writers and agents. That's a way you can get your foot in the door."

Sophie Green, publisher and commercial fiction author, episode 194

"Don't be impatient. As an agent and a publisher, so often I've seen people who get so excited, they've finished a draft and they send it in straight away. But that draft you've just finished for the very first time is never going to be the best representation of your work.

"It's better to sit on it for as long as you can bear, have another look at it and then send it in. Because when you send it to an agent or a publisher they'll only look at it once. Rarely will they look at it twice, so that's the only shot you'll get.

"Try to be patient and breathe. Then keep moving, get other ideas, keep those going. That's my number-one tip."

Louise Park, children's author and series creator, episode 189

"Join as many worthwhile industry organisations as you can. Through these organisations, you can get access to published authors who are willing to share their advice and their steps along the way. You can get access to publishers where you might be able to pitch a story or you might be able to have a session where you get feedback to help you continue working on that manuscript.

"They have a lot to offer. They offer really good courses. The Society of Children's Book Writers and Illustrators, the Australian Writers' Centre, the Australian Society of Authors – established places like these are invaluable.

"Join as many of them as you can and make use of everything they offer, because it will help. It will help you get out there and in front of the people you want to be in front of."

Pamela Hart, author and creative writing director at the Australian Writers' Centre, episode 242
"Workshop and draft your work before you submit it. Learn to take criticism, learn to be professional, learn to really listen to what people are saying about your work. And be prepared to make the changes that are necessary to make it better, because your book won't be published if it's not good enough.

"By that, I don't mean you're not talented enough. It's just that people go too fast. They write a first draft and then they send it off to the publisher. But only a handful of first drafts in the history of the world have been good enough.

"People have got to put the time in to do not just the first draft and the second draft and the third draft, but the eighth and the ninth and the tenth, if that's what's necessary."

Laura Sieveking, children's author and editor, episode 267
"Know the publishers well. Know what each publisher likes to publish so you can pitch appropriately. If you're trying to pitch a picture book to a publisher who doesn't focus on picture books, you've wasted time – theirs and yours. As a writer, knowing not just the market, but who's publishing what, is really important."

Eleanor Limprecht, historical fiction author, episode 253
"Be prepared for rejection, and be steeled for it. Writers are pretty sensitive souls, but people who have success as writers are able to get through that rejection. A lot of people give up and don't keep persevering. Persevere through the rejection."

Nicole Alexander, author, episode 184

"Be kind to yourself. Nothing happens overnight. If you're passionate about it, the result will be there for you. It's that old story – everyone says, 'Wow, life's a journey, it's the road, it's not the end result.' Well, writing is very much about that journey, so be kind to yourself along the way."

Marisa Pintado, children's and YA publisher, episode 182

"Really get to know the publishers you want to be published by. Follow them on Twitter, take note of which books are coming out, look for them in bookstores, read their books, find out what their tastes are like.

"Look in the acknowledgement pages, find out who published the book and see if you can build a really specific idea of the kind of person in publishing whose tastes might align with the manuscript you're trying to write, because that's one good way to find the perfect home for your manuscript.

"It will also save you the heartache of sending manuscripts to publishers who will never like it for personal reasons – not because it's not good, but because it doesn't fit with what they're trying to do."

Rachael Lucas, author, episode 166

"If you're going to write something, get it finished. Agents and publishers don't just want to see that you can write. They also want to see that you can follow through and actually finish writing.

"And you're going to have to finish another one if you're lucky and get a two or three-book deal. Finishing a book has to become something you get used to doing."

Louise Thurtell, publisher, episode 161

"I'm looking at a manuscript and thinking, 'Will this do well?' These days, you don't get a second chance. Well, you rarely get a second chance. A publisher has to think your first book can be successful.

"Sometimes you're able to increase an author's sales after a first book. It's just that it's really hard to sell it to the sales and marketing team that you want to do a book by that author again."

Rachael Craw, YA author, episode 138

"Learn to receive criticism. That's probably the lynchpin for developing your craft – learning to receive criticism and letting it make you better, rather than destroying you and rolling up in a ball and running away.

"This is the solid truth: I wanted to be good more than I wanted to be published – and I *really* wanted to be published. Having that dedication to your craft means you have to be willing to take your medicine. You have to be willing to swallow the hard truth and do the work."

Karly Lane, rural fiction author, episode 136

"Don't give up. It gets really depressing, especially if you've got to the point where you're sending out things and they're coming back – it sucks big time. There are times when you just go 'oh it's too hard' and throw it down. But then you've got to get back in there. And if they've given you some reasons, which they don't always, it's good to try to focus on that feedback."

Jay Kristoff, author, episode 127

"The odds in this game are remote, but you can do things to shorten your odds. Writing to current market trends is difficult, because by the time the book you're writing now gets published it's going to be two or three years' away. The trend you're writing to might be dead by then.

"It's important to understand broader trends – fantasy is a safe sell, for example – and understand the mechanisms that are in place to have books published.

"If you want to get published in America you probably need a literary agent, so you need to understand how agents work and how one acquires their services. Getting that grounding in the publishing industry and its mechanics was the first step."

Louise Doughty, author, episode 123

"I remember speaking to a publisher who said that, in his experience, it's quite common for somebody who has a kind of basic talent to need around seven or eight years of serious working at their writing before something falls into place. I think that's about right. Seven or eight years of trying and reading a lot and writing as much as you can before something clicks into place.

"If you think a doctor or a dentist or a vet takes how long to train? Seven years, for a lawyer. Writers need that same training period. You need to train yourself. You need to read and you need to often write a huge amount of not very good stuff, you have to get all of those bad sentences out of your system before you write something that can be published."

Fleur Ferris, YA author, episode 122

"Once you've finished a book and you've submitted it, just write the next book. Get yourself a portfolio of work. Do courses, speak to people and follow people's career who are already achieving what you hope to achieve. That was a huge learning curve for me, to follow those who were already getting published – Australian authors writing for the category I was aiming for."

Sue Whiting, children's author and former publisher, episode 109

"As a publisher, I often used to talk about the 'almosts', the books I almost published, and they used to break my heart. As a writer, I know how hard people work on their writing and their stories, and some of them might have been writing for years. They're good, but they just don't quite get over the line for whatever reasons.

"The advice I usually give authors is, 'Try not to be the almost.' When you submit your work, try to make sure you've got everything covered. Don't think that ending is almost right. Or, 'I know it needs some work in the middle, but it's nearly there.' Or, 'I know there are too many characters, but they can be edited out.' Don't give the editor the chance to have doubts."

Mitch Hogan, author and indie publisher, episode 89

"I finished the book and thought, 'Well, hang on, now I have this novel written, shouldn't I try and publish it?' So, I started querying agents and publishers and I did get some feedback from Rochelle Fernandez at Harper Voyager, but I ended up deciding to self-publish. I had an agent interested at the time, actually, but I decided to self-publish anyway.

"I really just wanted to get it out there. I wanted the readers to decide whether it was any good or not."

Meredith Curnow, publisher, episode 74

"Bookstores, be they online or the ones on High Street, are the best place to do research for writers who are looking to be published. You need to go into a bookstore, give yourself a couple of hours, half an hour perhaps if that's all you've got, just browsing the shelves, looking at books, looking in the section and just think, 'Where in this store do I want my book to be? Is it in the memoir, is it in health, is it in women's fiction, is it in literary fiction?' Then just look at the books around that and look at who published them.

"On the inside of a book, on the imprint page, it will give you full details of the publishing house, including their address. The acknowledgements page of a book is always a source of a lot of information. The author will often mention their editor or publisher – not always, but often they do. Note the publishing houses that you think are right for you."

Suzanne O'Sullivan, children's and YA publisher, episode 62

"Revise your work a lot, even if you're only writing a 200-word picture book. It really needs to be polished. Don't write something and then fire it off to a publisher right away. Put it in a drawer and come back to it two weeks later, have another look, see if there's anything that you could do better."

Sylvia Day, author, episode 53

"Every author has a theme, every author has a strength, every author has a weakness, and you have to recognise what those things are. For me, I feel it takes three novels to do that. I tell people to write three books and then think about publishing something.

"You'll have learnt so much about yourself and your style at the end of three novels that you'll be able to really put a work up for sale that's very reflective of you and something you can be proud of from now until you pass on."

Candice Fox, crime author, episode 48

"When I was starting out, I don't think I heard anyone saying, 'Put the book down if it's failed.' But that's my advice.

"If you've written it and you've edited it and it's gone to every single door and every single door has remained shut, put it down and do something else, because people re-edit at that point and then they re-edit and they re-edit and it's like getting a painting and just keep painting over and over. It just gets muddy and cluggy, you know? The original thing is lost. You should just start afresh.

"Every book is like a relationship. If it doesn't work out, don't keep flogging the dead horse, go and find someone else."

Bernadette Foley, publisher, episode 37

"I want an original voice. Now, that's different from an original story, because I really do believe that old saying that there are only seven stories in the world. It's not that you have to completely come up with a new storyline, but you do have to have a new way of telling it.

"Your unique voice as a writer has to come through, and I have to engage with that voice. It has to draw on my emotions, one way or the other. It either has to inspire me, or engage me, or interest me, or all of those things put together.

"I have to feel you're telling me a story that you really believe in. There's no use writing a romance story because you think they sell well. You have to really believe in it – the integrity has to come through."

The editing process

When you submit your manuscript to a publisher, that's not the end of it. In fact, for many it feels like just the beginning. Now comes the editing process. Everyone approaches this very differently. Some people love it. Others find it painful.

Regardless of which camp you fall in, rest assured that the editing process can only make your book better. And your editor only wants the best for you and your manuscript, so think of it as a gift.

Here are what some authors, editors and industry professionals say about editing.

Kylie Mason, freelance editor, episode 7
"Don't be scared of editors, and don't assume they're going to rip your book apart, because we won't.

"We might have questions about some of the choices you've made, and we might have suggestions about how to address those choices. But we're always going to take time to understand what you're trying to do with the story, and we'll use that understanding to help you improve the book."

Eliza Henry-Jones, author, episode 224
"Let your writing sit for as long as you possibly can. I'm still guilty of this – I'll finish something and immediately want to send it off. And you actually can't pick up on things.

"It's difficult to pick up on things in your own writing anyway. But the more time you give yourself between the writing and the reading, the more likely you are to pick up those typos, pick up the inconsistencies in the scenes, pick up all those little things.

"This is advice that's circulated a lot: just put your writing in a drawer. It's really hard to do – and it's so important."

Natasha Lester, author and creative writing presenter at the Australian Writers' Centre, episode 186

"Structural edits are always challenging. When you're writing the book, you're using the part of your brain which is just all imagination and letting that run away and run wild. And the structural edit is all about, okay, you have the story, and you have all the pieces of the book, and it's like a jigsaw. But you can just make each piece fit in just that little bit more neatly if you tweaked it the right way.

"It's very minute work, and very detailed work, and it takes up all of your available brain space for the entire time. My first lot of structural-edit notes from my publisher were 19 single-spaced pages long."

Hilary Spiers, author, episode 154

"Listen to everybody. Listen to your critical friends. Listen to anybody who reads your drafts. And listen to your editors. I feel readers know what they like to read, editors know what sells and what the market is interested in at the moment.

"I'm an absolute believer in that maxim 'kill your darlings'. My feeling is, 'If it stands out, then it sticks out.' And if it does that, you're trying too hard. I know it's difficult sometimes. You write something and you say, 'Oh, I'm really pleased with that.' But if you keep coming back to it and it snags the eye, there's something wrong with it. So you can bin that one. You can put that one in the bin, for sure."

Veronica Roth, YA author, episode 133
"I love revising. I'm not a big first drafter, because then you have to make a lot of mistakes and just move on, and that's hard for me. But I love finding the character, finding the story that you're really meant to tell and that you've built as you've gone along without realising it and helping it to come out more clearly and more compellingly than you did the first time.

"To me, that's the whole reason to do it."

Brandon VanOver, editor, episode 66
"The problem with some manuscripts is that they're workshopped to death. They go through writing groups. You're not working with an editor, but you're kind of editing – you're receiving editorial feedback that you're probably comfortable with because it's Sue down the street or Dan from university.

"They'll give you different opinions, and often conflicting opinions or vanilla opinions. The next thing you know you've ripped all the originality out of the manuscript.

"I often say I like getting just exactly what you did in its unvarnished self, because there's a lot of kind of originality and spirit and tension in that original manuscript that's often sucked out.

"Work with an editor instead. Being an editor is a trade – it's something you hone over time. It can really take your manuscript to places you hadn't imagined, and help you find your own voice within yourself and your writing."

Deborah O'Brien, author, episode 16

"Read your work out loud. Jane Austen used to read her novels to her sister, and my poor husband has to suffer this all the time. It's a great way of finding typos and clunky language and eliminating them. It also enables me to hear the rhythms, the cadences of the prose.

"I'd also recommend you read the book aloud at proofreading stage, just to check for final errors – it's a great way of finding them. If you just read it silently, you could easily miss them."

Building a writing career

Writing a book is one thing. Getting a book published is another. But building a writing career? That's a whole new ball game, as many debut authors discover when it comes to getting their next book published.

Fortunately, our author interviewees, many of whom are multi-published and with long-standing careers in writing and publishing, have kindly shared their experiences.

Karen Viggers, author, episode 273

"Learn to work with editors. Even if you don't agree with everything that they say, they have some distance from your work and can cast different eyes on it and see what is and isn't working and advise you on that."

Danielle Clode, author and academic, episode 229

"The thing I find most useful is to have a plan for what you're doing. And have more than one plan. You can have your grand plan of being an international bestseller, but have those littler goals on the list as well. Submitting to particular places, applying for fellowships, whatever it is, so you've always got something achievable to aim for."

Kerri Sackville, author and social commentator, episode 228

"Find your niche. Find what you love to write about. Find what you're passionate about. Find what you're excited about, and write about that. It sounds counter-intuitive, but the more niche you are, the more likely you are to find a place for yourself."

Jack Heath, author, episode 221

"Try to get a good agent. I never got anywhere until I had a good agent. When I wrote *Hangman*, my publisher didn't want it. I put it in a drawer and completely gave up on it. But my agent did not give up on it.

"She was submitting it to other people and collecting rejections. And not just rejections, but getting feedback that I could usefully use to transform the book. She was the one who eventually found a publisher for this thing that in the past no-one had wanted to touch."

Jackie French, author, episode 214

"Never believe your own press releases, and never, ever, ever say 'this is my style' and get furious at someone who says the book just doesn't work. You cannot fall in love with your own style, you cannot fall in love with your own words. You're not writing for yourself. If you want to write for yourself, write a diary. But when you write for other people, remember you're writing for them.

"You're not writing to show how intellectual you are, how clever you are, how much you've actually managed to transcend your disease or the horror of your childhood. You're not writing for yourself. You're writing for the reader. You're writing for the reader in terms of the theme, plot and the way you put the words on the page. And what you want is completely and utterly irrelevant. You're writing what they need."

Fiona McIntosh, commercial fiction author, episode 264

"The way I approach my writing is, I don't stress about it. I don't plot it or plan it. I just sit down and I write 1500 words today. Then I walk away and I don't think about it again until tomorrow. And tomorrow, I don't read what I wrote yesterday. I write another 1500 words."

Marisa Pintado, children's and YA publisher, episode 182

"It's definitely a bonus for us if we can see that an author is promotable and able to talk to students and at writers' festivals. If they present well, then of course that's a bonus. Having said that, we've also acquired manuscripts from authors who have zero online presence. There are particular kinds of publishing where being on Twitter is actually not as important as you'd think."

Zanni Louise, children's author, episode 169

"Nurturing your relationships and your community is very important. Find your comrades. I've got a couple of writers I'm in touch with on a weekly basis, and we're very supportive of each other's work and our journey, and it's a fantastic thing for me.

"Also, find your online communities, and your publishing contacts, and attend conferences. Don't exhaust those contacts, but nurture them and give back to that community.

"On my blog, I like sharing writing tips, I like sharing my experiences, and I hope that helps other people. Really being an active member of those communities will benefit you no end."

Tania McCartney, children's author and illustrator, episode 150
"Give back to your industry. A lot of people focus on their audience, so they write for their audience, they think about their audience, how they're going to get into their audience's ears, into their market's ears and eyes.

"I reckon flip the switch a little and think about getting involved in industry rather than worrying about your market. Because industry is your support.

"If you've got a brand-new book that you've written and you throw it into an ocean it's going to go 'plop' and sink. If you have a 10,000-strong industry behind you that you've developed genuine relationships with over 10 years, who rub your back when you rub theirs, who love and support your work, you throw that book in that ocean and it's going to make a splash.

"Opportunities, support, networking, collaboration – all of these things come with focusing on the industry, sharing what you know, sharing your knowledge with others. They'll share it with you. You'll grow so rapidly and you'll have incredible, outstanding opportunities if you can do that. So focus on the industry."

Katherine Johnson, author, episode 128
"It's a really hard game. Even though you have one book published, that doesn't mean the second one is guaranteed to be published, or the third one. So you have to love doing it – you have to really enjoy the process."

Kylie Scott, romance author, episode 112

"The hardest thing with writing a series is not letting your brain get lazy. If you read three books in a row by an author, you'll often see they kind of have a recipe. There's a map that they follow.

"Make sure your plot points are different and your themes are different in each book. Critique partners are invaluable for this."

Emma Allen, picture book author, episode 99

"I needed to get some confidence that what I was writing had some merit, and everyone has different ways of going about that. For me, it meant going back to university and studying literature – doing it the long way. But that's given me such a great freedom now, because I feel that when people ask me what I'm doing with the book or with the story or with the words, I can really respond in a professional way.

"I've learnt so many valuable skills, like how to work on a text and how to not feel discouraged if it's not working out, and how to reapproach it and renegotiate it, and all of those things."

Hazel Edwards, author, episode 96

"Choose a subject you actually care about – if you don't, it's going to show through. I don't believe hack writers can survive. I do not believe writing what everybody else wants or everybody else is doing because you want to make a million is going to work, it just doesn't work. You need a unique voice on something that really matters to you."

Mary-Rose MacColl, historical fiction author, episode 80

"Everybody in writing thinks the next thing will be the thing that makes them happy. It seems to be a career like that. I've been a little bit successful as a writer and I've been incredibly unsuccessful over time as a writer. I don't think either of those things ultimately improved my writing or made me happier as a person. What's made me most happy is actually playing with words and going off into a story.

"The fact that people read what I write is a bonus, but the journey has to be why you do it. It's too hard to do it just for ego."

Nicole Hayes, YA author, episode 60

"I remember thinking, 'I need to engage with people, I need to learn from other people and find out a bit more about how things work from other people.' From other writers really.

"I have no idea if I sold more books because of it, or if I'll sell more books because of it, but the feeling of community I've managed to cultivate as a result of social media – really just Facebook and Twitter for me – has been incredibly satisfying.

"It's emotionally and psychologically very helpful, but it's also resulted in paid work, which I didn't expect."

Annabel Smith, author, episode 56

"Think of writing as a long game and try to enjoy the process. When you're first writing, it's all about getting your book published – that's the holy grail. That's wonderful, those moments are amazing, but it's about the journey, not the destination.

"There are lots of ups and downs. You have to try to enjoy all of the parts of it. You have to enjoy the writing, and you have to enjoy getting out there and sharing your book with people. You have to try to embrace all of the different aspects of it."

Rachael Johns, author, episode 41

"If you're writing romance, my biggest tip would be to join Romance Writers of Australia. There are about 900 members, some published, some not. They run conferences and have newsletters, contests and a great community too, where you can talk to other writers and get tips and feedback. That was the biggest thing for me."

Bernadette Foley, publishing veteran, episode 37

"Ask questions. Publishers have the best intentions in the world, but like anyone who's been doing their job for a while we assume a lot of prior knowledge, which we shouldn't do, but we just do.

"If you can't understand why something is happening, why there's a delay or why you haven't heard from someone in a while, just email or get on the phone. We underestimate the importance of just picking up the phone and talking to each other."

Favel Parrett, author, episode 35

"I was surprised by the feeling of embarrassment from public reviews. It's so weird because you've got this terrible feeling like everyone you know in the world has read this review, if it's not such a good one. You have this deep, like, 'Oh my god, I've exposed my soul and I wish I could take it back.' It only lasts for a short time, like a day or two, but it can be excruciating."

Kylie Ladd, author, episode 32

"It's not a glamorous life. It's not glamorous at all. There are glamorous moments – they're lovely, those moments, but they're not the sum total and they're not all that common either. A lot of it is sitting in my pyjamas or my tracksuit pants with the holes in them and wanting to beat my head against my desk.

"I find writing to be hard work, and I often wish I didn't feel obliged or compelled to write. That said, the relief and the joy I feel when I have written – and I feel in myself that what I've written is okay, can be made to work, is going to be all be good – is wonderful."

Liane Moriarty, author, episode 25

"Don't read your reviews. You probably will, and there will be at least one that hurts.

"One way to make yourself feel better is to think of a brilliant book by an author you adore. Then look up the one-star reviews of that book. You'll feel better for at least five minutes."

Kim Wilkins, author, episode 15

"Be prepared to diversify. Don't say, 'All I ever want to write is paranormal romance for teenagers,' and never vary from that. Be prepared to explore other aspects of your craft and your creativity. Then you've got more of a chance of writing success."

Graeme Simsion, author, episode 100

"I don't plot as I go. I plot first, and I have a complete plot laid out on cards, on physical cards, index cards, as screenwriters are fond of doing, before I put anything much on paper. I might write a chapter, just to get a sense of the voice and whether it's going to work and so forth. In the case of *Adam Sharp* I wrote a short story, as a precursor. I think it's a great way of working up a character. So, I had a bit of a sense of what I wanted to do there. But, then I went back, I got the entire plot sorted out and then started again.

"When I write, it doesn't mean the the plot is set in concrete. I will go back and modify as I go, and sometimes a story will take me in a different direction. You're never purely a plotter or a pantser."

R.A. Spratt, children's author, episode 268

"If you're a writer and you get a book deal, or you've got your first foot on the first rung, the number-one tip I give people – and they never listen to me, but this is the number-one tip I've been giving people for 20 years – is to get yourself an entertainment accountant.

"Get an accountant who knows about the business, because it's going to be different. The entertainment business is different to any other business."

Nicole Hayes, YA author, episode 146

"It's a tough gig, that's for sure. Don't get into it for the money, that would be my first advice. Write something that you love or that matters deeply to you. Because it's a long process if you're going to write a book.

"You need to have something you connect with in a really powerful way, to push through those tough, lonely days. But also because, at the end of it, that's where your authenticity comes through. That's where the best writing comes through."

Wendy Orr, children's author, episode 134

"If you can work part-time and have some form of outside income, that can actually help your writing. Because to write anything really good, you have to be prepared to fail badly. You have to experiment.

"Now, there are lots of people who certainly make much more money than I do, sell many more books, and they don't take this advice. They've honed what they want to do, and they do that, so it's a personal thing. But I believe that you want to go on experimenting.

"*Dragonfly Song* was a huge risk. It was very different to what I'd done before, but it was something I felt I really had to do. So I believe a little bit of outside income helps you write what you want.

"I mean, failure is horrible. You pour your heart and soul into a book and it flops. It's horrible! But you have to be prepared to risk it."

John Birmingham, multi-genre writer, episode 118

"I divide my work time between long form and short form, so the books I write are a separate business line from the media work I do. The books are really the main earner, because if a book goes off it's going to earn an enormous amount of money.

"But also there's a great freedom with writing books. You're not immediately answerable to an editor, you're not trying to fit within a house style, you don't have a deadline tomorrow morning. A book is due – specifically, if you're self-publishing – when you want to put it in.

"There's a great quote, and I can't recall who it's from, but it says, 'No work of art is ever finished, it's merely abandoned.' That's very true of books – you just eventually give up on them and hand them over to the publisher."

Mitch Hogan, author and indie publisher, episode 89

"Know what your goals are, why you want to write, what you want to get out of it at the end. Do you just want your print book on the shelf of a bookstore? Or do you want to make a living? Or do you want to win awards?

"There's writing, and then there's the business of writing. You really need to understand both, and if you don't then you're doing yourself a disservice. As an author, you're essentially a small business. You're trying to make money and trying to make a living out of your writing – at least, that's my goal."

Ellie Marney, YA author, episode 88

"Get a platform so you can communicate with your readers. Whether that platform is on Twitter, Facebook, Instagram or something else, find something that makes you feel comfortable, and then you can branch out from there."

Emma Noble, book publicist and author, episode 83

"Know what your book is about. A big mistake authors make is not understanding what their book is actually about. Be able to describe your book succinctly and clearly in one or two sentences."

Danny Parker, children's author, episode 81

"Don't hold onto your words like they're your children. Really, don't. You've just got to be prepared sometimes to tell the story in another way if you want someone to read it."

Jacinta di Mase, literary agent, episode 71

"I'm looking for manuscripts that engage, entertain, inspire. Or at least two out of three. For authors, I want to see evidence of reading widely and knowledge of the current market in your genre, and that you're connected in the industry. That you're a member of a writing group, an active member of Romance Writers of Australia if you're a romance writer, or the Children's Book Council of Australia if you're writing for children. Or the Society of Children's Book Writers and Illustrators, or the Australian Society of Authors.

"There are so many ways of being connected, and interested, and informed. That's important to agents because the relationship is a collaborative one. We're actually working together to get the best results for an author or illustrator. Working with someone who's connected and motivated, and not just sitting back and hoping everyone will tick the boxes for them – it's more rewarding if you work together, and you definitely get better results."

Annabel Smith, author, episode 56

"There are lots of parts of the writing life that are beyond your control. So you do the very best you can with the parts you can control and then you have to try to make peace with the parts you can't control.

"There's no sense in spending energy saying, 'It's not fair,' and, 'Why did this book get celebrated when it's so mediocre?' and, 'Why did this person get a grant when they're so obviously untalented?' That's a trap you can get into of getting bogged down in aspects of the industry that you have no influence over.

"It's better to just say, 'That is how it is. Here are the things I can work on, and I'm going to put my focus there.'"

John Purcell, author and bookseller, episode 5

"Ensure that you've got some commitment from your publisher to market you and to present you. An easy tip is that I'd ask the marketing or publishing people whether or not they can get a banner for your book onto one of the big websites, or get a poster made if you want to get it into shops."

Read like a writer

Once you become a writer, you'll never read in the same way again. At least, very few writers we know do. The reason is that you'll be forever analysing plot points, considering what literary devices were used and assessing whether the pace should have been faster or slower.

It's an occupational hazard – and one that we suggest you get used to. Sure, there are times when you can lose yourself in a novel so much that you don't notice any of these things. And if you're able to do that, great!

However, we believe it's better if you hone this skill and read like a writer whenever possible. You'll learn so much from the process. These professionals share how this skill helps them with their own writing.

Kirsty Manning, author, episode 240

"I'll be in bed reading and I'll whip out a sticky note and write 'great character foil' or 'ooh, upending of a mystery!' or 'great red herring'. I sticky note all my books as I read."

Jaclyn Moriarty, adult, YA and children's author, episode 209

"People used to say 'read a lot', and I'd always be reading my favourite style and genre of book and favourite authors. Then I realised that the key is in reading outside your favourite style and author, outside of the style and genre you're writing in – reading non-fiction, science and history, and poetry.

"Because I usually write for young adults, I read a lot of books in that genre, but I find it's really important also to read science fiction. And often I notice I read books by women, so sometimes I'll try to read something by men for variety. Non-fiction, science, history and things like that can really trigger your imagination in unexpected ways.

"If you're writing a kids' book, reading literary books is important to remind yourself of all the possibilities that are out there, because you should never be writing down to children."

Marisa Pintado, publisher, episode 182
"I divide my reading into two styles. I have my work reading, which is a very active kind of reading. I pay close attention to every word and the flow and structure of every sentence, because I'm interested in the technical aspects of how to make a book good, how to make a story good.

"But I have another kind of reading, which is flow reading, where you just read to make pictures inside your head, to be entertained and to go into new worlds.

"I'm reading Terry Pratchett at the moment and that's my flow reading, and it's awesome. So you can do both, but sometimes you need to do active reading to get the most out of it."

For freelance writers

When you start out as a freelance writer, you're constantly seeking information. How much should I charge? What is a pitch? How do I get an editor to read my pitch? How do I find case studies for my stories? So many questions...

The best way to get those answers is, of course, from the horse's mouth. That's why we always recommend a course, and always recommend looking at the teacher of that course very closely. You need someone with first-hand knowledge of the industry – and not just the industry in general, but current industry practices.

As a starting point, however, you can't go past our podcast interviews with journalists, freelance writers, editors, content writers and other industry specialists. These tips offer just a hint of what you can learn from them.

Getting started

Sarah Keenihan, science writer, episode 125

"Building up your networks is the critical thing. Starting off, you need to work out a way to get yourself known. I'd suggest for anyone considering a transition to a science-writing career that they take it slowly. You're not going to hit the ground running immediately.

"Just start taking on one or two clients and then build it slowly and make sure you show your face, physically and through social media and all of the places that clients might be.

"Go to events, live-tweet from the events, learn how to use hashtags appropriately to hook up with the right people. Find out who matters in science writing in the place you live, or who does the kind of work you want to do, and ping them regularly."

Donna Webeck, real estate writer, episode 230

"I don't condone working for free, but if it's the only way you can get a couple of things in your portfolio, then it's worth it. Then you can start showing potential clients, 'Hey, this is what I'm capable of, this is what I could do for you.' And then you might have a business born."

Sue White, travel writer, episode 217

"The first thing that's really important to remember in travel writing is that it's not the same as going on a holiday. You can't just go on your next holiday and come back and write a story and have done nothing different while you're there. Editors are not going to be interested in that.

"With a travel-writing piece, you should feel that the experience of being away, or even that experience of researching in your own town, is somehow different to what you'd do in your normal life. You're going to be talking to more people, you're going to be interviewing.

"You won't be going to the same beach in the Maldives every day. You'll be going to all the different beaches. You're not going to eat in the same restaurant you just love every night. You're going to be moving around and getting different experiences. And of course, you're going to keep your eye out for really good angles, so you can sell multiple stories."

Getting the story
Kirsten Galliott, editor, episode 36

"If you've done your research and you're going into the interview knowing a lot about that person, then you can't really go wrong. But you need to really do your research – read quirky bits and pieces about the person and add that into your interview. It just gives you so much more colour and you get a much better result. And the subject will give you more because they appreciate the effort you've gone to."

Sarah Keenihan, science writer, episode 125

"Sometimes if I'm doing a particular story and I talk to a specialist, we'll talk for 30 minutes just to get that golden quote. A lot of what they say I understand, and it helps inform me in writing the article, and to look for other places for information. But then only one sentence that they say is actually appropriate to be in the article. So, it can take time."

Sue White, travel writer, episode 217

"When you live somewhere, when you're local to somewhere, you often have fantastic insider tips. And those are what make a really good travel writer. They're what make us different to a brochure or to Google – we've got that inside scoop.

"It's really sensible to start looking around your local area and think, 'What story opportunities are here that I could do that would be low cost, or I'm paying to do anyway?' Because we're all forking out for all sorts of things. Figure out how they could potentially be turned into a story."

Bernadette Schwerdt, copywriter, episodes 43 and 262

"The people who make great copywriters are curious. They don't just stop with, 'What do you do?' They go, 'But why did you become that?' And then, 'What do you like about being in that occupation?'

"They absolutely drill down, because they're keenly interested in other people. They're keenly interested in popular culture, what's going on in the news, what's going on in world politics."

Writing your story
Kirsten Galliott, editor, episode 36

"Know what to cut. One thing that drives editors crazy is asking for a 2000-word article and getting a 4000-word article. You should be able to take a step away from it – take a day's break if you have to – and come back to it and know what doesn't work or what is extraneous.

"Work on your hook and make sure your kicker is great as well. Don't just let your story float away at the end. Come on, slam it. You've had someone with you on a journey for 2500 words – make them love the end as well."

Sarah Keenihan, science writer, episode 125

"Audience awareness is one of the most important parts of science writing. Imagine a news story online: the detail can be there and available to people who are interested in the detail, but it can't be upfront because you're going to scare people away.

"It needs to be interesting and relevant and suck people in early, and then you can link to more detailed information or have it further down in the piece as well, if there's room.

"Keeping the audience front of mind is absolutely critical, whether you're working in the broad news environment or within an academic environment."

Bernadette Schwerdt, copywriter, episodes 43 and 262

"Writers of novels and creative writers are actually very well cut out for copywriting for one really good reason, and actors too. They're people who are in the business of channelling.

"Think about when you're writing stories and you've got characters, you're living that character. You're absolutely embedded in that character's emotional world. The ability to do that is very related to copywriting, because you've got to walk a mile in the shoes of your customer."

Kate Hennessy, corporate writer and music and dance critic, episode 82

"For an album review, you've only got 150 words. I try to not only get across the ideas, but I want every verb and adjective, every word I use – even the flow of it – to reflect the feel of the album."

Specialist writing
Sarah Keenihan, science writer, episode 125

"Even though you're a science writer, you can't just know about science. You must see that science sits within a broader culture. You have to know what people are watching on TV. You have to know what kind of audiences you might be trying to tap into. Don't shut yourself off into a little science bubble. You have to read broadly, use Facebook, watch crap TV."

Donna Webeck, real estate writer, episode 230

"Every house has its own individual angle, that something that makes it special. If the owner is there, I'll talk to them and ask them three questions. What do they love the most? What will they miss the most? What's been their favourite time in the house?"

Bernadette Schwerdt, copywriter, episodes 43 and 262

"You don't need to do a degree to become a copywriter. You just have to understand marketing and have the flair for words."

The business of writing
Donna Webeck, real estate writer, episode 230

"Make sure every client feels like they're your number one, because there's competition in real estate. They're all in competition with each other. But I always have that inner hope that I make each of them feel they're just as special to me as everybody else."

Sue White, travel writer, episode 217
"Good travel writers will understand how to take one destination and turn it into a multitude of angles."

Bernadette Schwerdt, copywriter, episodes 43 and 262
"There's a sea of content out there. We're drowning in it. The content that's going to rise to the top and get results that the clients want has to be written in a way that gets the result. If you can't do that, the clients are going to go to someone who can."

Kate Hennessy, corporate writer and music and dance critic, episode 82
"With corporate writing, you've got to deliver something really, really good every time, and you've almost got to pretend your byline is on it. A lot of corporate writers get a bit lazy because there's no byline – it's not attached to their name. You can't do that."

A wealth of wisdom

So there you have it. A treasure trove of advice from many of the writers we've interviewed. They've shared it so that you can learn from their mistakes and follow your writing journey more confidently, and without having to second guess yourself.

We're big believers in standing on the shoulders of giants. So take in their advice, climb on up – and enjoy the exciting view of what's ahead of you!

CHAPTER 14
So now what?

If you've reached this chapter, we already know you're going to make it. Yep, the tyre-kickers don't get this far. They make excuses way back in chapter three and find all sorts of reasons why they can't read on. And soon they'll be telling you all the reasons why they can't find time to write.

That's not you. If you follow the advice in this book, you'll get there. The speed at which you'll get to your final goal will be determined by how frequently you take action.

And on that note, just remember: run your own race. Everyone is different, everyone has very different goals and priorities, so don't compare yourself to how someone else is going.

Consider only *your* goals and decide your own pace. Sometimes you'll go hell for leather and your momentum will be in full swing. At other times you're going to get bogged down with that crazy little thing we call "everything else in life". And that's okay too. Remind yourself that this is totally fine.

We know you'll be able to find the information you need. We know you'll find the right course or community to help you along. This chapter is not about writing techniques or industry advice, but an overall approach you need to succeed.

It's about your mindset.

It's vital to think about your mindset and attitude if you want to achieve anything. We touched on this at the start of the book, but we're mentioning it again because this will be the cornerstone of your success.

The first thing we want to talk about is the fact that you need to decide where you want to be with your writing. That's about setting goals, whether they're big or small.

If you can already see where you want to be 10 years from now, fabulous! You can work on setting the smaller goals you need to reach in order to get there.

If you can't see past simply getting your first-ever article published, that's fine too. Work towards that and, once you achieve it, think of your next incremental goals.

We're not here to tell you what your goals should be – you'll need to work that out for yourself. But we want to encourage you to have some.

Your goals can change. Don't fret and think, "Oh, I really need to pick my goal carefully because I must choose the right one." That's just procrastination. Even if your goal is a bit vague, that's okay. Just go with that for now.

You can always evolve your goal. It's better to get moving in *some* kind of direction – and course-correct along the way – than not move at all. Some kind of goal is better than none.

If you don't have a goal, you don't have direction. And if you don't have direction, then you kind of just wander around at a loose end and don't get very far.

Once you do have a goal, you can work out what action you need to take to get there. Sometimes this will be obvious. If your goal is to get your first article published. or to get to four articles (or more) published per month, then you'll need to pitch a certain number of ideas.

With other goals, the steps might not be quite as obvious. That just means you need to figure out what they are. If you want to get into copywriting, you might do a course. Perhaps it would also be a good idea to talk to other working copywriters. Remember what we said about "having coffee"? Find out how they get their work and what kind of copywriting work is out there.

Even when you do this – when you work out the steps you need to take to achieve your goal – this can still stump some people. They can create that list of action steps and intellectually they *know* this is what they need to do. But they can feel disconnected from it.

This may or may not be you. If you're confident about moving forward, go right ahead. Don't wait. Stride forward in the direction of your dreams!

But you might look at your list of things to do and just feel… *Will it really work? Can I really achieve my goal? Will this list of actions really lead me to achieve my writing dreams?*

Let us assure you that this is perfectly normal.

Part of it is because you could be wondering whether these steps really do lead to success. To that, we say that we've seen countless success stories from writers who were once in the position you're in.

They followed the advice in this book and achieved exactly what they wanted. They've seen their bylines appear in print or online. They've published their novels. They've transitioned out of corporate jobs and into new careers as writers. Or they've kept their day jobs because they love them, and they have a nice part-time income from their writing.

We know this works. When you take action, *it works*. Not when you take half-arsed action. Not when you only do one thing on your To Do list and need to do five things to achieve your goal. If you take action, stuff happens!

We know that most of the time you just need to give yourself permission to pursue what you want. After all, you don't have to get it from anyone else!

That's how Sarah Bailey felt when she first started writing. Sarah was an advertising executive who was secretly passionate about writing.

Simply allowing herself the opportunity to follow her passion was a huge first step for Sarah. "It was a little bit about permission. When you're not a professional writer, you can become convinced that any time you spend writing is self-indulgent, even selfish. Structured courses can help you feel more purposeful and you meet other writers, which helps to legitimise the cravings."

Sarah completed a creative writing course at the Australian Writers' Centre. "It helped me fall in love with narrative all over again. It made me really think about writing as a discipline and in some ways as a science," she says.

"I walked away from the course feeling incredibly determined. I went from wanting to write a novel to *deciding* to write a novel. It helped me to feel like I had a right to spend more time writing.

Most importantly, it inspired me to create my own world and get the words down."

Since then Sarah has published the multi-award-winning crime thriller *The Dark Lake* and its sequel *Into The Night*.

Imposter syndrome

The other factor that could be causing you to doubt whether you'll make it is when imposter syndrome creeps in.

We started this book by talking about how important it is to believe that your writing dreams – no matter how fanciful they are – can come true. Fundamentally you need to believe it's possible to achieve what you want. This is such an important tenet that we're going to say it again. Because this self-belief is at the core of your journey.

If you don't believe it can happen, you're putting an obstacle in your path even before you start. That doesn't mean you won't achieve it – sometimes we achieve our goals despite our self-limiting beliefs. But it does mean it will be *harder* to achieve your goals. And why make things hard for yourself?

Equally, if we don't fundamentally believe we can achieve our goals, we often just don't take any action. It's easy to think, 'Oh, it's a pipe dream anyway so why should I pitch to that editor?' Or, 'Why would I go for that writing job that's everything I want? I know I won't going get it anyway.'

There's a famous saying that we miss 100 per cent of the shots we don't take. If you don't take action – because you don't believe your dream will come true – then of course you're not going to get anywhere. At all!

We know you might read this, understand it intellectually and still not be able to shake that feeling of self-doubt. You'll tell us you want to believe it, but that you secretly don't. For whatever reason.

We get it. And we're not here to offer you years of therapy to get over it.

Well, you can go through years of therapy if you want, but that's a very time-consuming and expensive way to get there.

Instead, you can make a decision.

You can make a decision to *allow* yourself to believe you're worthy of this dream. To allow yourself to believe you can achieve this goal. To allow yourself to believe you can make it happen.

It's a decision. And you can make it in an instant.

If you're still not convinced, just let this message brew for a while. Sit with it for a while.

Because who are you *not* to have this goal? If this is something you want, you can do it.

We've given you lots of suggestions on where you can find support, a great community who will cheer you on, teachers who can show you the craft, and more.

Once you really believe you can achieve your goals, it's just a matter of time and implementation. Just take the action that you've identified you need to take to get there.

Self-doubt might creep back in if you then have a bigger goal. And then a bigger goal. That's normal. It's imposter syndrome coming back to visit again.

Because, guess what? Imposter syndrome never fully goes away. That's right. It never disappears. Sometimes it's right next to us and we can be debilitated by its presence. At other times, when we're feeling more confident, it's on the sidelines – but it's ready to pop right back into the picture when we least expect it.

I realise that's bad news for some. But it's great to understand and accept that this is the case. If you wait for imposter syndrome to disappear, if you keep your dreams on hold until you believed you've banished it forever, you'll never come close to making your dreams comes true.

So what do you do to cope?

Feel the fear – and do it anyway

Feel the Fear and Do It Anyway is the title of a fantastic self-help book by Susan Jeffers. In essence, it's all about taking action – no matter how doubtful, anxious or downright scared you might be.

For our purposes, we've adapted this saying into three main points.

When you feel self-doubt creep in, when you can tell you're about to succumb to the paralysing phenomenon brought on by imposter syndrome:

1. Acknowledge that feeling. Acknowledge that it's there. That you might be thinking, "Who am I to do this? *Can* I really do this?"
2. Once you acknowledge it, understand that it's normal and it's not going to go away. Sometimes it affects us a lot. Sometimes it affects us a little.
3. Then feel the fear – and do it anyway.

It's point three that will keep you moving in the direction of your dreams. Self-doubt will *always* exist. So when you want to take action but are racked by fear, just take the action anyway.

So now what?

Seriously, what are your choices? You can either:

- feel the fear and let it stop you from achieving your goals, or
- feel the fear and move towards your goals.

The first option leads you nowhere. But with the latter, you have nothing to lose – and everything to gain!

Let yourself shine. Don't hide the creative spark that you know is within you. Don't be afraid to own that you want to be a writer.

Stop letting your fear keep you a prisoner.

Like the engineer who recently told us that all he really wanted to do was write but was hesitant to really give it a go. Instead, he just played around on the edges, penning the occasional stories but not feeling good enough to share them with anyone.

Or the graphic designer we spoke to who was in her forties and still so afraid of pursuing her dreams because of what her mother was going to think.

And then there was the secretary who told us she wanted her hopes and dreams to "remain hopes and dreams" because she suspected she wasn't actually any good at what she really wanted to do. And she didn't want to take the risk in case she found out for sure.

Who cares whether you're good at it or not?

Chances are, you *will* be good at it anyway. But if you never give yourself a chance, you'll never discover your amazing potential. You'll deprive other people of the pleasure of appreciating what you create or write. And you'll never experience the creative joy you really deserve.

We know that fear is sometimes the result of naysayers – whether they're our former teachers, our parents or our friends.

It's important to realise that most of these naysayers usually don't mean to be negative. They don't realise that what they say can be hurtful and discouraging, that their genuine and well-intentioned concerns can crush our dreams.

It's vital to think about the way *you* respond instead. You're in full control of that.

You can choose to let other people shape your life. Or you can grab your destiny with your own hands. Don't hide your passion or talent.

Let that spark inside you shine.

It's our greatest wish that you pursue your creative passions and that you achieve whatever it is you want with your writing. We know you can do it. We hope you do too.

And we hope you enjoy the journey!

About the authors

Allison Tait

Allison Tait (aka A.L. Tait) is the internationally published bestselling author of two middle-grade adventure series, *The Mapmaker Chronicles* and *The Ateban Cipher*. A multi-genre writer, teacher and speaker with more than 25 years' experience in magazines, newspapers and online publishing, Allison lives on the south coast of New South Wales, Australia, with her family.

Race to the End of the World, the first book in *The Mapmaker Chronicles* series, was published by Lothian Books (Hachette Australia) in October 2014. It was shortlisted for the Readings Children's Book Prize 2015 and named a "Notable" book in the CBCA Children's Book of the Year Awards 2015.

Book number two, *Prisoner of the Black Hawk*, was released in April 2015 and was shortlisted for the 2015 Aurealis Awards (Best Children's Fiction). Book number three, *Breath of the Dragon*, arrived in October 2015, with book number four, *Beyond The Edge Of The Map*, published in April 2017.

The Mapmaker Chronicles series is available in Australia, the USA, the UK, Lithuania and Turkey.

The Book of Secrets, book number one in the *Ateban Cipher* series, came out in September 2017 in Australia, with *The Book of Answers* (number two in the series) following in March 2018. Both books are also available in the USA, through Kane Miller Books.

In recent years, Allison has shared her passion for writing and creativity at numerous events for children and adults, including Singapore Writers' Festival, Brisbane Writers' Festival, Sydney Writers' Festival, Somerset Celebration of Children's Literature and more, as a speaker, workshop facilitator, chairperson and panellist. She's a regular speaker in schools, and is represented by The Children's Bookshop Speakers' Agency.

Allison is the creator of several courses for the Australian Writers' Centre, including Make Time to Write, Creative Writing 30-Day Bootcamp, Build Your Author Platform and Creative Writing Quest for Kids.

Allison is a board member of the Shoalhaven Readers' and Writers' Festival, and is the current director of the children's program. In January 2019, she received a Shoalhaven City Council Australia Day Award for Outstanding Contribution to Arts and Culture.

Valerie Khoo

Valerie Khoo is founder and CEO of the Australian Writers' Centre (AWC), the country's leading centre for writing courses. The centre has evolved into a hot-house for talented writers, who are regularly selected by major publishers for book deals.

She's a mentor to freelance writers through the AWC's innovative masterclass program designed to nurture freelance writers to build a lucrative and rewarding career.

Valerie is also a keynote speaker and author of *Power Stories: The 8 Stories You MUST Tell to Build an Epic Business*. She regularly presents workshops for corporate and consumer groups on communication and creativity.

Valerie has spent 20-plus years in the world of writing and publishing, including 13 years writing for the *Sydney Morning Herald* and a range of glossy magazines. She has previously worked as a public relations consultant and began her early career as an accountant at PwC and lecturer at the University of Sydney.

She now combines her love for writing with her creative pursuits as a visual artist. Valerie is also curator of the Sydney Lunar Festival, the City of Sydney's arts and culture festival, which attracts more than 1.4 million people.

Both Allison and Valerie are co-hosts of the top-rating podcast *So You Want To Be A Writer*.

Acknowledgements

This book is the product of two lifetimes of writing experience. As such, the list of people we have to thank for bringing us to this point is long and lustrous and would take an extra 30 pages to fill. So, in the interests of saving your eyes from strain, we're going to keep it short and sweet.

Valerie and Allison would like to thank the writers of all genres who've given up their time and experiences for our podcast interviews, the thousands of listeners who've banded together to form the wonderful *So You Want To Be A Writer* podcast community (look us up on Facebook – yes, really, do!), and the incredible team at the Australian Writers' Centre who help us bring the podcast to you. And thank you to Nigel Bartlett and Linda Diggle for your help in getting this book done.

We'd also like to thank the hundreds of amazing people we've worked with during our writing and publishing careers, our friends and families for their support and understanding, and our various four-legged writing companions who offer us unconditional love and a non-judgemental (albeit fluffy) ear when we try out new ideas.

Connect with us

We'd love to share your journey as a writer!

Search for *So You Want To Be A Writer* in iTunes to find our top-rating podcast, or visit writerscentre.com.au/podcast to listen via the website and other options.

Find Valerie
Website: valeriekhoo.com
Twitter: @valeriekhoo
Facebook: @valeriekhoo.33
Instagram: @valeriekhoo

Find Allison
Website: allisontait.com
Twitter: @altait
Facebook: @allisontaitwriter
Instagram: @allisontaitwriter

Find the Australian Writers' Centre
Website: writerscentre.com.au
Twitter: @writerscentreau
Facebook: @writerscentre
Instagram: @writerscentreau

So you want to be a writer?

Then you NEED our free weekly newsletter! Arriving in your inbox every Thursday, it's filled to the brim with writing tips, opportunities, competitions, industry news, insider info and much much more. A must-have resource for any writer and regular burst of motivation for you each week.

And pssst – sign up today, and you may also find an exciting surprise waiting for you ...

Special bonus

We know by reading this book, you're serious about your writing. And we want to help you smash your goals. By subscribing to the AWC newsletter at **writerscentre.com.au/signup** you'll be rewarded with a special bonus to give you the momentum you need.

*"Most of my emails will be deleted without viewing, some will be reserved for dealing with later, and a few – very few – will be read immediately once they arrive. The **AWC newsletter** is one of these very few."*

– Penny Burns

*"I must say **AWC is one of the rare newsletters I read regularly** (and sometimes even file for future reference!)."*

– Sharon Halliday

*"Thank you for your weekly newsletter! I read it every time and find it **useful, fascinating, entertaining and educational.**"*

– Robert Scriba

Join our awesome community and grab your exclusive offer today. Go to **writerscentre.com.au/signup**

Happy writing!

Made in the USA
Las Vegas, NV
17 November 2021